D0501651

ELECTRONIC DEMOCRACY

"... one of the curious problems of democracy is the result of the development of the electronic media ... We used to think of the conscience as being a private, intimate, still, small voice within. Now the conscience of democracy becomes the whole community sitting in the livingroom watching what has been done."

—Daniel Boorstin

ELECTRONIC DEMOCRACY

TELEVISION'S IMPACT ON THE AMERICAN POLITICAL PROCESS

ANNE RAWLEY SALDICH

FOREWORD BY BERNARD RUBIN

PRAEGER SPECIAL STUDIES • PRAEGER SCIENTIFIC

Library of Congress Cataloging in Publication Data

Saldich, Anne Rawley.
   Electronic democracy.

   Bibliography: p.
   Includes Index.
   1.   Television in politics—United States.
2. Political participation—United States. I. Title.
HE8700.7.P6S24   320.9'73   79-18592
ISBN 0-03-052146-7

Published in 1979 by Praeger Publishers
A Division of Holt, Rinehart and Winston/CBS, Inc.
383 Madison Avenue, New York, New York 10017 U.S.A.

© 1979 by Anne Rawley Saldich

All rights reserved

0 038 098765432
Printed in the United States of America

To Virginia Thompson Adloff

FOREWORD

Bernard Rubin

Electronic Democracy is a provocative, insightful analysis of television's impact on politics and government in the United States. Anne Saldich, a political sociologist who specializes in broadcasting, is sharply critical of the commercial networks when she thinks they misuse society's most persuasive medium, but she also thinks that television is one of the greatest democratizing forces in American history. The author's flair for going beyond muted clinical observations to concrete events makes her commentary clear and cogent. Her goal is to distill the political lessons that ought to be learned from television, particularly from its coverage of such traumas as Vietnam, Wounded Knee, and the Chicago riots in 1968.

When Dr. Saldich refers to television as a corridor to power she is describing a less romantic and mystical medium than what Marshall McLuhan, that acclaimed prophet of the 1960s, made it out to be. Saldich does not aim at acceptance as a seer, or as a darling of the advertising fraternity who took McLuhan to their hearts. She is concerned with fundamentals. In well documented essays she challenges network executives for usurping governmental functions, teaching a politics of violence, and neglecting opportunities for public service.

Television has become the major image-machine, depicting political participation. For those who depend on TV as a sole source of information it tends to confuse rather than inform. Although television provides daily news to millions of people, minorities complain of invisibility, and crucial government issues are presented so vaguely that viewers are trained to be cynical not only about their representatives but about democracy itself.

Quantitative analyses and cautious conclusions by scores of researchers seldom go beyond absolutely verifiable, limited data. The results are often fragmented and misleading. Communications specialists who are enamored of scientific methodology, in this computer age, tend to ape colleagues in the physical sciences by focusing on separate pieces of the puzzle whereas Saldich boldly attempts to unveil overarching patterns. That is the appropriate task of a careful political essayist who appreciates both the constructive and destructive power of television.

The author realizes that when message-makers are democratic and well-intended the chances for social construction are high. Unfortunately, good intentions are often sacrificed even by advocates of constructive change if one is unaware of public needs, or the nuances of TV's persuasion. Remember that old complaint about the best candidate having lost while the most telegenic won? Remember how much we were told on TV but how little we learned about the Kent State University disaster? Remember how we were glued to the TV news year after year during the "Vietnam" War, learning less and less that made any sense? We know that television can transfer information but it alone cannot inspire citizens or leaders to do what is right when they turn off the tube. Television educates but drowns its education in entertainment. It entertains but provides all sorts of accidental education. It seduces with innuendoes about the good life. It tempts with its barrage of prosperity images. It aggravates by dramatically magnifying the problems we face. It pretends that there are simple solutions to complex issues. Nevertheless, television can establish national solidarity and community when talented educators, entertainers or advocates use the medium effectively.

Electronic Democracy is a welcome addition to the literature. Anne Saldich dares to analyse what traditional researchers timidly ignore. She uses her training in political sociology to shape new perceptions about relationships between television and the future of democracy. Her research conclusions are important. Her ideas need to be considered not only by media specialists but also by the general public. She is grappling with a powerful reality, not playing around with clever rhetoric about a "medium cool." Dr. Saldich knows that media realities directly affect the quality of democracy in America, for good or ill.

Bernard Rubin
Director, Institute for Democratic Communication
and
Professor of Governmental Affairs and Communications
Boston University

PREFACE

Television is a great democratizer. As a corridor to power for people who are excluded from the political system, it has revitalized the body politic. Although voting statistics show fewer citizens going to the polls for periodic elections, television shows more participation in the political process and by a wider spectrum of people on a continuing basis. But TV teaches a politics of violence. It has documented time and again that physical assault and property damage attract the cameras which, in turn, command the attention of authorities who often ignore more orderly petitions.

Despite superficiality of coverage, television news and public affairs programs have the highest credibility of all media and are the principal sources of information for most Americans who follow the news. For the majority of those people it is a sole source of information. This may be good news for the networks, but it is bad news for democracy where the quality of political action is determined by the quality of knowledge on which that action is based.

Broadcasters now exercise governmental functions but without the checks and balances characteristic of American democracy. For example, "gatekeeping," a traditional governmental function, determines who will have access to the public. Today it is in the hands of broadcasters. Even presidents are denied access to the viewing public by network executives. Similarly, the nation's political agenda used to be set by public leaders. Now it is decided by broadcasters who control which facets of politics will be reported and which will be ignored. The networks shape political values and politicize people who might otherwise be apolitical. Television has restructured the political process by weakening parties and conventions, personalizing power, increasing campaign costs, and nurturing a sense of community among similar groups that are geographically separate, poorly organized, and who were hitherto powerless politically. Television is a part of government's decision-making process because it reaches the nation instantly, simultaneously, and visually. This unique political power must be factored into cost-benefit analyses of alternatives that the government considers when formulating policy.

The similarity between tyranny and television is no longer secret. Both are highly centralized in that a handful of people decide what millions will see, hear, and think. Televised information lacks diversity and flows in one direction, which is another characteristic of tyranny. Yet, it is often accepted at face value. Although TV's narrow base of decision makers has access to the largest audience among all media, there was an absence of accountability until 1968 when Vanderbilt University's Television News Archive was established.

Although our Founding Fathers could not foresee that the American press would grow from penny sheets to powerful institutions, they did know that the best way to guard against tyranny is to divide, check, and balance power. An effective way to do this is to teach electronic literacy. Viewers must learn that what they see is not always what happens, that television is not a neutral conduit of information, that it is no more objective than any other medium, that it can distort reality intentionally as well as accidentally, and that it is an inadequate source of information on which to base political action.

Several antidotes to television's political power have already evolved. They include television archives, which are as important to electronic democracy as the public library and school systems were to the linear era when print dominated democracy; viewers' pressure groups, which are forcing stations to make program changes; press councils, which monitor programs and mediate disputes; technological innovations, such as cable, satellite, microwave relay, fiber optics, and lasers, which may temper network monopoloy of video audiences.

Television's impact on the American political process is well-known among communication specialists. But it should also be considered by the general public if substantive policy changes are to be made. It is for that public that this book was written. For clarity, I should say that my use of the term political process encompasses pressure groups and their labyrinths of influence that affect American political life. It is not limited to campaigns and voting or to the structure and function of political institutions.

ACKNOWLEDGMENTS

This study was privately funded by Bob Saldich, who encouraged every facet of the research during these past several years. I am grateful not only for his generous financial support but also for his help in countless other ways. The project's spiritual director is my friend and former professor, Virginia Thompson Adloff, Distinguished Scholar in Residence at the Institute of International Studies, University of California, Berkeley. Dr. Adloff helped me to define the scope of this subject, and her continuing interest has sustained me throughout the writing. My son, Alan, patiently listened to many long passages and commented on their readability, for which I thank him.

I am particularly indebted to people who gave me interviews: *Commercial Networks:* at NBC News—Sid Eiges, Vice-President of Public Information; Reuven Frank, Vice-President; Julian Goodman, Chairman; J. Ronald Milavsky, Director of Social Research. At CBS News—William Leonard, Senior Vice-President and Director of Public Affairs; Gordon Manning, Senior Vice-President. Richard Salant,* President. At ABC News—William Sheehan, Sr. Vice-President.

Public Television: James Day, National Educational TV; at KQED in San Francisco: William Osterhous, General Manager; Zev Putterman, Producer; Don Roman, Producer, Joe Russin, News Director.

Office of Television Policy (Nixon Administration): Henry Goldberg, General Counsel; Clay Whitehead, Director.

Television News Archives: Karin Ades* Public Information Coordinator, Public Television Library; Erik Barnouw, Chief, Motion Picture and Recorded Sound Division, Library of Congress; Dr. Alexander Heard, Chancellor, Vanderbilt University; James Moore, Director, Audiovisual Archives Division, National Archives, Washington, D.C.; James P Pilkington, Administrator, Television News Archive, Vanderbilt University; Paul Spehr,* Assistant Chief, Motion Picture and Recorded Sound Division, Library of Congress; Paul Simpson, Founder, Television News Archive, Vanderbilt University; Samuel

---

*Telephone interviews.

Suratt, Archivist, CBS News; Leslie Waffen, Motion Picture and Sound Recordings Branch, Audiovisual Archives Division, National Archives.

Other Interviews: Professor Paul Goldstein, Stanford University Law School; Professor Phil Jacklin, philosopher and media activist, San Jose State University; Professor Seymour Martin Lipset, sociologist; Mark Lane,* attorney for the Indian activists at Wounded Knee; Congressman "Pete" McCloskey, U.S. House of Representatives; Reverend Everett Parker, media activist, Telecommunications Office, United Church of Christ; Ned Schnurman, Associate Director, National News Council; honorable Joseph Sneed, deputy U.S. Attorney General in charge of the government's Wounded Knee negotiations; Tom Tyson, video activist and graduate student, who made on-location films about Wounded Knee.

Thanks to the criticism of several readers, this book is more error-free than it might otherwise have been. I am deeply indebted to: Elsie Begle, Professor Thomas Blaisdell, Judith Pillman Bredhoff, Douglass Cater, Kirke Comstock, Professor Gladys Lang, and Sara Molla. I appreciate their generosity in taking time from busy schedules to review the text, though I am ultimately responsible for its content.

Terry Nasta has my special thanks: Because of her intelligence, competence, and excellence as project editor this publication process has been a pleasurable experience.

---

*Telephone interviews.

CONTENTS

Foreword
  by Bernard Rubin   vii

Preface   ix

Acknowledgments   xi

1
McLuhan Revisited: A "Cool" Medium Heats Up the Viewers   **1**

  Indochina: The "Vietnam" War   4
  Wounded Knee, 1973   11
  The 1968 Democratic National Convention   18
  Appendix: 2/28/79 Letter from Richard Salant to Dr. Saldich   20

2
How TV Governs   **22**

  An Overview   22
  The Dynamics   23
  A Unique Political Power   25
  TV and the First Amendment: Government Regulation   26
  Immediacy versus Civic Order   28
  Impact on Linear Illiterates   29
  State Censorship   30
  Political Television   31
  Problems   36
  Reshaping the Political Process   38

3
Democracy and Television   **49**

  Old Myths and Their Realities   49

Low Voter Turnout and Interest Politics 50
Politicizing Linear Illiterates 53
An Informed Citizenry? 57
A Court of Last Resort 59
Creating the News 59

4
Television and Tyranny **61**

From Penny Sheets to Powerful Institutions 61
Television, Tyranny, and Democracy 63
A Tyrant Tyrannized 66
Televised Tyranny? 67
Media Cross-Ownership 68
Linear Illiteracy, TV, And Political Power 69
Distorting Reality 71
Belief and Power 73
Television and Behavior 74
Government Control 75
Accountability 77
Political Reality and TV 79

5
Personalizing Power **80**

Intimacy and Political Credibility 80
Presidential Television 82
Public Broadcasting and Government Propaganda 86
People Power 88

6
Watergate: A National Civics Lesson **92**

Precedent 92
A National Civics Lesson 93
Televised Coverage 94
Authority and Credibility 95
"News Management" 96
Honesty in Government 97

7
Broadcasting Enters an Era of Public Accountability **100**

Access and Accountability 100
Television News Archives 101

Compiled Subject Tapes: CBS Control of Government
    Archives Policy   106

8
Policy Considerations   **110**

Bibliography   113

Index   119

About the Author   123

ELECTRONIC DEMOCRACY

1

McLUHAN REVISITED
A "Cool" Medium Heats Up the Viewers

Marshall McLuhan soared to fame in the early 1960s when his ideas about the impact of media on people and society caught the public imagination and swept through this country like wildfire in a high wind. His *Gutenberg Galaxy* created a sensation, and two years later when *Understanding Media* came out, he was already a legend and the leading communications guru. In 1967, *The Medium Is the Massage* crystallized his thought and focused on one of his central beliefs: media are as important as their messages. Said differently, form dominates content. He thought TV subtly massaged viewers into passivity because it gave them vicarious experiences that allowed the same emotional release as if they actually had participated in an event.

People argued over McLuhan's writings with a religious fervor worthy of cabalists. A vast literature grew, analyzing what he said, what he did not say, and what he intended to say. McLuhan's ideas were revolutionary because he distinguished media and their impact from message content. He was interested particularly in the unifying force of electronic communication and enjoyed calling the world a global village whose values were shared by virtue of the

---

The televised news coverage for the cases in this chapter was reviewed by borrowing video cassettes from the Television News Archive (TNA) at Vanderbilt University in Nashville, Tennessee. This research would have been impossible if TNA did not have an excellent index and provide the technical service of splicing together video clips to make compiled subject tapes. Editorial decisions that guide the making of subject tapes are the user's decisions, not TNA's.

media. This is erroneous, actually, though perhaps not conceptually, because most of the world's population is not exposed to modern media. Newly developing countries comprise the bulk of the world's population, but not all of them rely on radio, television, and print journalism to disseminate information. In China today wall posters are a mass medium. This is far from what McLuhan had in mind because his global village connotes instant communication. However, one of his ideas still has considerable impact. He believed that television does not incite people to act because it is a "medium cool." In practical terms, this absolves broadcasters of responsibility when it comes to violent behavior, for McLuhan argued that TV defuses rather than causes violence.

Violence is a subject that TV covers well, whether it is ritualized in sports, fictionalized for drama, or erupts spontaneously. Although you actually can sit at ringside or the 50-yard line, be present at the scene of a riot, a revolution, a murder, or have center aisle seats in the theater you rarely can see action with the same clarity that TV viewers can; close up, in living color, complete with replays from a variety of perspectives. For years experts have wondered if there is a causal relationship between televised violence and violent behavior. And for years TV executives have defied common sense, insisting that their medium portrays but does not cause violence. They claim this in spite of the fact that the average 18-year-old has spent more time in front of television than in the classroom, with TV getting 15,000 hours as opposed to 12,000 school hours during those same 18 years. During that formative stage of life, an average child saw 18,000 murders and countless incidents of rape, torture, robbery, arson, and beatings. If we are supposed to believe that this has no negative effect on behavior, we should also believe that people are unaffected by positive values in the home, church, school, and at work and play. But we do not believe this because systematic analysis as well as casual observation show that people respond well to decent behavior. What a comfort it must have been for network managers when McLuhan came along and gave television his absolution as a cool medium, instead of saying that it catalyzed action.

Television has been around long enough for us to have some measure of historical perspective. From that vantage the view of violence is clearly discouraging. Numerous studies cite TV as a significant factor in antisocial behavior and many people believe that McLuhan's medium cool is plenty hot. With supporting data in hand, the public has started to organize political pressure groups. Some have succeeded in forcing the industry to reassess its policies. Among the most effective activists are Action for Children's Television, the American Medical Association, Citizens' Committee on Television, Committee on Children's Television, National Citizens' Committee for Broadcasting, the Parent-Teacher Association, and the United Church of Christ. The result? We are beginning to see some restraint on the intensity and kind of televised violence, and on the hours at which violent programs are shown. Broadcasters tried to substitute violence with sex, but they received a lot of criticism for that as well.

Actually, television is neither cool nor hot. It is both. However, for our political analysis it is useful to review McLuhan's definition of cool in *Understanding Media*:

> There is a basic principle that distinguishes a hot medium like radio from a cool one like the telephone, or a hot medium like the movie from a cool one like TV. A hot medium is one that extends one single sense in "high definition." High definition is a state of being well filled with data. A photograph is, visually, "high definition." A cartoon is "low definition," simply because very little visual information is provided. Telephone is a cool medium or one of low definition, because the ear is given a meager amount of information. And speech is a cool medium of low definition, because so little is given and so much has to be filled in by the listener. On the other hand, hot media do not leave so much to be filled in or completed by the audience. Hot media are, therefore, low in participation, and cool media are high in participation or completion by the audience. Naturally, therefore, a hot medium like radio has very different effects on the user from a cool medium like the telephone.

McLuhan goes on to say that television is a timid giant because it does not handle hot history (current events) well. "As a cool medium TV has introduced a kind of *rigor mortis* into the body politic." This causal relationship between technology and passivity is given a political context in a passage where McLuhan refers to radio as "The medium for frenzy" and compares it with television (1964): "Castro's use of TV has cooled Cuba down, as it is cooling down America. What the Cubans are getting by TV is the experience of being directly engaged in the making of political decisions." Here, McLuhan is referring to televised tirades in which Fidel Castro harangued his audience for hours on end with tireless energy. McLuhan's point is that Castro gave viewers the feeling of participation in the political decision-making process.

To put McLuhan's idea of a medium cool more simply, we can think of television as having three characteristics. The first is low definition, which simply means that there is not a lot of detail given to viewers, much the way that artists minimize detail in caricatures or comic book frames. The effect is simplicity, unlike film, which can handle complexity better because movie screens have more space in which the action takes place. By contrast, the TV screen is small and tight. Television cameras therefore focus on the subject to avoid confusion, and a lot of detail (what McLuhan calls high definition) is supplied (imagined) by the audience. This brings McLuhan to his second point: television requires participation, but the participation is vicarious, which causes the third characteristic: cool. Because TV involves more than one sense, it intensifies vicarious experiences and satisfies (cools) the need for actions.

The political significance of a cool medium is that its low definition requires political simplification. This ties in with McLuhan's idea that TV is not suitable for dealing with hot history and controversial topics. After an event cools down or a controversy becomes more manageable, TV is an appropriate vehicle for distilled information. McLuhan's idea of participation is brimful of political implications because his participation is passive. It is not unlike the catharsis that one experiences when watching a film or play. The emotional release of tension can be so profound that one feels like a participant in the drama instead of a mere spectator. Similarly, viewers are so caught up in the TV program that any inclination to participate is anesthetized by vicarious experience.

There are some spectacular examples of vicarious participation to support McLuhan's thesis. One is the coronation of Queen Elizabeth II, which was broadcast and transmitted to people throughout the world. The funeral of President John F. Kennedy partially realized McLuhan's global village: millions were united in grief by electronic technology. Another example is the space program. Television transcended geographical, national, linguistic, and political barriers when the first man walked on the moon. It was a moment of shared pride in human achievement. Because of television, each event had a dramatic you-are-there quality and the audience participated emotionally, but was not moved to act. This was television as medium cool.

TV became hot during the era of street politics in the 1960s, when people from all socioeconomic levels took to the streets in protest to attract public support for their beliefs. Initially these demonstrations were peaceful, but as time went by they had an unsettling tendency to become riots, with the good guys and the bad guys clearly portrayed, as in TV westerns. Demonstrators usually had no weapons and were often clubbed, maced, or strong-armed by authorities, so they were the good guys. It took awhile for people (including journalists) to realize that protests were often staged for TV, that violence sometimes was planned into the demonstration because television producers like action shots, and that the police sometimes got as good as they gave when it came to a roughing up. Increasingly, TV became a catalyst for action among viewers as well as demonstrators. To illustrate this point three cases will be discussed: the "Vietnam" War, Wounded Knee, and the 1968 Democratic National Convention.

INDOCHINA: THE "VIETNAM" WAR

During the early years of America's Indochina War, the federal government's press, functioning under the guise of public relations, easily misled reporters and, through them, the American people. Those years of misinformation had such devastating effects on the United States that it is instructive to consider how the government press and the free press interact.

Because America's forebears feared censorship as an instrument of tyranny, they did not ratify the Constitution, which had been written in secrecy, until a long and public debate yielded the Bill of Rights: ten constitutional amendments, the first of which guarantees freedom of the press. By law and tradition, we think of the media as private institutions, separate from the state, representing the complete spectrum of political and social thought. The bulk of their profits comes from advertising. Public broadcasting (radio as well as television) is an exception to that general rule: it is not funded by commercials because there are none. User subscriptions, corporations, philanthropic organizations, and the federal government underwrite public broadcasting. It, together with commercial broadcasting and the print media, comprise America's free press. However, there is another well-financed, state-owned, mixed media that functions in the United States, but Americans are reluctant to admit that much of what passes as government public relations (PR) is what it is: state-controlled journalism. Yet the evidence is compelling. Millions of people are employed by the U.S. government not only to inform but to manipulate public opinion. The source of their funding is the House of Representatives. The power of the purse is in this branch of government, which allocates tax money for governmental activities, including public relations. Therefore, the House of Representatives has a responsibility to insist that government-originated information is labeled as such. Often it is not.

Government PR can rightly be called a working press because its products are the same as those of the free press: books, articles, films, documentaries, newsclips, tapes for TV and radio, pamphlets, and newspapers such as the military's *Stars and Stripes*. Government journalism is not confined to software. It also includes the means of production and distribution: the Armed Forces Radio Station, Radio Free Europe, the Government Printing Office, superbly equipped radio and TV studios in the White House, Congress, and Pentagon, and the U.S. International Communication Agency, formerly the U.S. Information Agency (USIA). The scope and purpose of the government press activities were analyzed in an excellent CBS documentary, "The Selling of the Pentagon" (1971).

Unfortunately, the media's role in relationship to the government press is not admirable. Too often it is one of gratitude for free or low-cost handouts that fill space or air time. But the worst aspect of it is that many media managers do not reveal the source of these fillers.

It is said that countries have the kind of press they deserve. If so, we should pay attention to how America's is evolving. During the past two centuries the U.S. government has gradually, almost imperceptibly, increased its power over compiling and disseminating information so that its publications now permeate the free press. Media executives have behaved scandalously in using government information without identifying it. This is an insidious encroachment on the First Amendment. It is journalists and broadcasters themselves who are undermining their own institutions in this regard. Government fillers are not the problem. The threat to democracy comes from using them without identifying the source.

America's war in "Vietnam" is an excellent vehicle for analyzing the interrelationship between government and the mass media. Even the name testifies to government PR's effectiveness, which conditioned us to call it the "Vietnam" War despite the fact that it was not, by any stretch of the imagination, confined to one country. The war encompassed Laos, Cambodia, North Vietnam, and South Vietnam—which comprise Indochina. War breeds deception, not only of the enemy but often of the folks back home.

When President Kennedy needed money for U.S. military personnel in South Vietnam, they were described to the public as "advisers." Since there was no declared war between the United States and North Vietnam, it would have been unseemly to have "soldiers" in South Vietnam. Later, when it became obvious that U.S. "advisers" were combatants, the word "war" was avoided in favor of "military intervention" or "small conflict." As "conflicts" intensified and the financial drain on tax dollars became increasingly heavy, Congress was given the ultimate sales pitch: our American "presence" was needed "to keep South Vietnam safe for democracy."

That the Vietnamese did not want democracy (they wanted peace) and that their leaders wanted political autonomy were not mentioned to American taxpayers who financed this war. That democracy is a political system that has been rejected by many countries for ideological reasons, and that it will not work in most others because they do not have the prerequisites to support it (high literacy, meaningful political campaigns, good communications systems), were not mentioned either. That "to keep South Vietnam safe for democracy" meant dropping more explosives on three small countries than the Allies had dropped in Europe and Asia during all of World War II was not dwelled upon at any great length, nor were the dead and wounded. Nearly 57,000 Americans died between August 4, 1964 and January 27, 1973. Most were painfully young, barely adults. In that same period there were 153,329 American injuries, people who were wounded in the prime of life. Many will never see or walk again. Many have spirits that are crushed, minds or limbs that are gone forever. One may argue that U.S. leaders who requested public monies for the "Vietnam conflict" could not have foreseen these figures. But surely it occurred to someone that war is more than cashflow?

One may argue that America's increasing involvement and the duration of our "military intervention" were not anticipated. How could the U.S. have known? Our politicians, statesmen and women, our military leaders could have read history and learned why the French failed to keep Indochina as a colony. America could have profited from puzzling over why France's well-trained, well-equipped, modern armies were defeated by an "underdeveloped" nation that was predominantly illiterate, by people on bicycles who walked or pedaled along jungle trails and mountain paths, by poorly equipped Asians whose ingenuity, tenacity, and determination were rooted in a desire to control their own destiny and in a belief that they would beat the French.

It is the free press, as distinct from the government press, that is America's self-declared watchdog, the U.S. version of Britain's loyal opposition that asks hard questions and demands government accountability in the public interest. However, few American journalists went to Indochina before 1964. Most did not even know where it was, much less what the United States was doing there. If reporters probed too ambitiously, government PR people pulled out the stops and soothed them with doubletalk.

The PR experts explained away challenges: graphs, charts, statistics on the "body count" showed that more of "them" died than us. Therefore, the United States was winning, or doing a brilliant job of advising the South Vietnamese on how to win (depending on whether the United States admitted to "advisers" or combattants). In short, the extensive resources that the American government had at its disposal to mask U.S. involvement were overwhelming. Reporters easily were manipulated since they had to have military permission for everything from transportation to entering combat zones. It was easier and less costly for journalists to accept official handouts such as press releases, completely written news stories, photographs, statistical data, and film footage. It was all available, courtesy of their friendly U.S. government. Much of the material that Americans saw on television about the United States war in Indochina during the early 1960s was used by the media without viewers knowing its source was governmental.

If Watergate gave us the journalist-as-hero, the early years of America's Indochina "experience" gave us, with few notable exceptions, the journalist-as-dupe. That changed in the late 1960s and early 1970s, partly because foreign colleagues of American war correspondents filed stories that ran counter to what U.S. reporters were told at the government-run afternoon press conferences. These were known as "The Five O'Clock Follies" because that was the time when military officers were scheduled to meet with, and sometimes lie to, reporters. As we learned later, these public information officers and their superiors also lied to Lyndon Johnson, their commander in chief, the president of the United States.

Let us consider the massacre at My Lai. It is an example of how the military lied to the government, and then how both manipulated public opinion in a country that is world renowned for its free press. Americans did not learn about My Lai until 20 months after it happened. Certainly it was a "newsworthy item," as they say in the trade, that in March 1968, "On a routine search and destroy operation a company from the America Division had walked into the village of My Lai and without provocation had gunned down three hundred and forty-seven civilians, most of them women and children. A photographer had taken pictures of screaming women, dead babies, and a mass of bodies piled up in a ditch." (Fitzgerald 1972) This "incident," along with U.S. tolerance of torture and arbitrary political imprisonment by the South Vietnamese, was hidden from American journalists. It might not have come to light at all except for the moral courage of Ron Ridenhour, a U.S. helicopter door gunner, who heard about it and decided that it was important for Congress and the American people to hear about it, too. And so, in a leisurely, circuitous way, rather than through vigorous investigative reporting by the press, the ugliness of America's "involvement" gradually oozed into the open. But government PR had been so skillful that for a year and eight months the freest press in the world successfully was deceived. By that time, in 1968, the networks alone were spending $5 million a year to cover Indochina, and there was a corps of 500 journalists, from all media, assigned to the war zone. Only Washington, D.C. had a larger number of reporters in one bureau. (Small 1970)

The American public's response to My Lai was shock and dismay. People did not want to believe that "our boys" were guilty of war crimes. And, as has happened since time immemorial, there were efforts to kill the messenger that carried those sad tidings. Many military and government representatives were furious with the U.S. press. Accusations were made that the report was a media fabrication, that journalists were unpatriotic because the report gave aid and comfort to the enemy. Governmental and civilian investigations paralleled each other but the facts would not go away. Disillusionment set in. Gradually America faced up to this and other atrocities for which U.S. personnel were directly or indirectly responsible, and the press became increasingly vigilant.

Once the facts about My Lai were made public, the immediacy of electronic reporting made it impossible for Americans to believe in a favorite myth, that the United States is supermoral. Although North Vietnam was guilty of similar heinous crimes, that did not mitigate American atrocities. In any event, the enemy's inhumanity was seldom seen by U.S. reporters to write about or to film, and this vacuum etched more finely the disillusionment that Americans at home felt about a war abroad.

America's war in Indochina was never a declared war, despite a 12-year "presence." Therefore there was no official censorship policy since censorship is legally permissible only during a declared war. Perhaps this explains an erroneous assumption on which Peter Braestrup based his two-volume study of the 1968 Tet offensive: *Big Story* (1977) is a valuable source about a narrow slice of the war and how it was reported. One of his themes is that there was no American censorship. Leonard R. Sussman, who wrote the "Introduction," is unequivocal:

> The Vietnam experience decisively changed the relationship between the press and the American government. The adversarial aspect of that relationship, normal in peacetime, received its first modern wartime test under conditions of no censorship . . . large segments of the public did not understand—and some bitterly condemned—the extension of press freedom to the battlefield.

To be equally unequivocal: this statement is false and misleading. There may not have been complete censorship, but there was censorship and a lot of it. It took the form of self-censorship by military personnel, who knew about or partici-pated in atrocities like My Lai; it manifested itself at military press conferences and during interviews in deliberate attempts to mislead the American public through civilian reporters; it showed up in assigning a military "escort" to Ron Ridenhour (who broke the news about My Lai) when he returned to Indochina as a journalist. (*New York Times* September 28, 1970)

Censorship means excluding unacceptable facts, feelings, ideas, and impulses. One can make the definition more complex but, essentially, that is what it comes to. One may give it other names: "embargo" was the Nixon administration's preferred term in 1971, but that does not change it. The military did not have any censors in Indochina but they had soldiers called information officers, some of whom eventually protested that they were permitted to write only favorable news releases and that they were reprimanded for volunteering unfavorable information to civilian reporters. (*New York Times* January 5, 1970) Isn't that censorship? How about distorting facts? It was reported that the U.S. military phonied up statistics on helicopters and casualties. Helicopters that were shot down were not listed as lost if their wreckage could be retrieved. ("CBS Evening News with Walter Cronkite," February 22, 1971) We do not know how much wreckage had to be retrieved to translate "lost" into "not-lost." Would two propellers do? As for Laos, American soldiers who died there were recorded as having died in Vietnam because President Nixon gave his televised assurance to the American people that only South Vietnamese soldiers would invade Laos. So, of course, no Americans could die there. But ABC reported that some American "advisers" went into Laos with the South Vietnamese forces, and its network showed film of a helicopter picking up four dead Americans. A fifth dead soldier appeared to be American but was dressed in a South Vietnamese uniform. That news program closed with a report from the administration that there were no U.S. troops in Laos. ("ABC Evening News," February 3, 1971) Is denial of filmed facts censorship? There are many more examples one could cite, such as the February 3, 1971 CBS evening news program when Walter Cronkite reported that news organizations appealed to the White House to lift what the Nixon administration called an "embargo" on news about the invasion of Laos. Isn't "embargoed" news the same as "censored" news?

My Lai became public toward the end of November 1969. Five months later President Nixon announced that the U.S. was invading Cambodia. The nation shook with protest. During an antiwar demonstration at Kent State University in Ohio, four students were shot to death and nine were wounded by National Guardsmen. Ten days later two students were killed and 12 were wounded by state police in an antiwar demonstration at Jackson State College, Mississippi. The press was unsparing in its coverage and TV was the hottest thing going: it taught demonstrators in various parts of the country what they could expect by way of repression from authorities and how to cope with it. TV dramatized an urgent need to protect our constitutional right to dissent. Violence abroad. Violence at home. The reaction was furor.

After Jackson State, 130 colleges suspended classes for a week and some, like Princeton, for the rest of the academic year. On May 9 a vast community of demonstrators (estimated between 60,000 and 100,000) gathered in Washington, D.C. Their message was not just that they wanted an end to the war. Their overarching concern was that America's democratic commitment to human rights was compromised severely at home because of our policies abroad.

During that long, hot summer of 1970, television recorded the wreckage on campus after campus: broken windows valued in the range of $50,000 to $80,000, at one university, alone; buildings aflame; antiwar graffiti scrawled across anything that smacked of the Establishment (the Bank of America's windows were smashed so often in Berkeley, California that management gave up repairing them: they simply bricked over the window space); destruction of Reserve Officers Training Corps (ROTC) quarters; mob scenes when military-oriented companies came on campuses to interview students for employment; draft cards publicly burned; teach-ins to bring out facts about the war that the government tried to hide or chose not to discuss. TV recorded and disseminated all this, the hottest of hot history, and did it well. This was an era when traditional authority was undermined: its representatives, its symbols became objects of scorn and ridicule, not reverence—the American flag was defiled frequently.

The Cambodian invasion was followed, nine months later, by a U.S. "incursion" into Laos, which took place while the government simultaneously shipped American troops home from Vietnam. The United States had given up the idea of unconditional victory in favor of "peace with honor," the Nixon administration's euphemism for "defeat." Interestingly enough, the public's reaction to Laos was unpredictably quiet despite extensive and aggressive television coverage. There were few protest demonstrations. One could almost see TV journalists searching for their proper role. In reviewing ABC's nightly news during the month of February 1971 when Laos was invaded, one notes a kind of counterpoint between Howard K. Smith, whose editorials minced no words in their support of President Nixon, and Harry Reasoner, whose skepticism, even cynicism, is captured eloquently in a strong editorial on February 25 when he satirized an American general who implied that one had to be a military officer "in order to see the big picture" and appreciate just how well the war was going. Part of Reasoner's retort included a comment on the administration's games with statistics, and its relentless insistence that American troops were not in Laos. Said Reasoner: "If you are eighty feet off the ground, in a helicopter, and you have been shot, there is little interest in whether you were on the ground or not." The alternation between Smith's support of the administration and Reasoner's hard-hitting criticism reflected an awareness at ABC of the enormous responsibility that TV has to present balanced reports and editorials without reducing the news to blandness. During the same month of February 1971, the CBS and NBC evening news programs also were focusing on military misinformation and doubletalk, which brought into question the government's credibility, which is the keystone of democracy as it is for all other governments. But this phase of the "livingroom war" did not throw the nation into turmoil in spite of strong visuals and scathing analyses. It was an example of TV as a cool medium

Why, with Laos, was there a reaction so different from Cambodia? If anything, the TV reports were more aggressive. Was it because of the timing? The Cambodia invasion took place in April 1970. This is a time on campus when student spring fever finds release in raiding one another's dormitories and generally letting off steam. Did Cambodia feed into the rites of spring whereas Laos, occurring in the winter, fed into a new semester when students are usually earnest about getting their work off to a good start? Did the eerie quietness tie into the economic recession, reminding students that they had better be serious about academic work if they wanted jobs when they graduated? Was it because some of "our boys" were on their way home and it looked as if the United States would get out of the morass of an undeclared war? Had Americans become inured to television war and administration doubletalk? Was it simply that the protest about America's invasion of Cambodia had effected so little change? We may never know the precise answers. The fact is, the medium hot of Cambodian days was a medium cool during Laos.

WOUNDED KNEE, 1973

American Indians are one of the most disadvantaged minorities in the United States. They have been so ever since their conquest when, herded like cattle onto often infertile reservations, they were compelled to live in squalid idleness as wards of the state. For years the U.S. government's policy of benign neglect amounted to little more than warehousing human beings, and history passed them by. Even black slaves were granted citizenship long before the Indians, whose first ballot was not cast until 1924. No longer confined to reservations, some Indians have integrated successfully with the rest of society, but a large majority choose to remain where they are. After two centuries as social outcasts most of them passively accept their poverty and despair. Low self-esteem and hopelessness have broken the spirit of a once-proud people.

When Wounded Knee became a public issue in 1973, reservation Indians earned an *average* per capita annual income of $1,100. Their *average* unemployment rate was 40 percent, compared with a national average of 4.9 percent. Not infrequently, several children and parents lived in one-room tarpaper shacks without plumbing or electricity, as if the United States were an underdeveloped country instead of a leading producer-consumer of the world's goods and resources. Alcoholism, tuberculosis, infant mortality, and suicide rates were alarmingly higher for Indians than for the rest of the nation, while life expectancy was several years less. The federal government's Bureau of Indian

Affairs (BIA) was supposed to care for the Indians, but statistics support those who contend that the BIA was ineffective.

Life among the Oglala Sioux on the Pine Ridge Reservation in South Dakota reflected this social profile with one significant exception. There, a small group of Indians actively opposed the government-endorsed tribal council, which they thought of as an instrument of the BIA rather than representative of Indian interests. In January 1973 these dissidents invited members of the militant American Indian Movement (AIM) to Pine Ridge for the purpose of trying to improve social and economic conditions through political means. A month later, convinced that legal methods were fruitless, AIM decided on dramatic action and forcibly took over Wounded Knee, holding several people hostage. This hamlet, located about 18 miles from the village of Pine Ridge, consisted of some 70 houses, a few churches, and a white-owned trading post. For symbolic and historic reasons, Wounded Knee was an obvious platform from which to stage a civil rights protest because it is the infamous site of the last recorded Indian resistance. There in 1890 the Seventh Calvary slew 200 Indians, women and children included. Their common grave is an indictment of white oppression and evokes memories of Indian courage.

Armed with handguns, rifles, shotguns, and at least one automatic weapon, AIM laid seige to Wounded Knee in February 1973, ransacking the store and taking prisoners who were later released. But their objective was larger than theft or kidnapping. It was political, a bold attempt at media politics to force authorities into giving Indians their civil rights. AIM was dominated by radicalized, urban Indians who interpreted white values as materialistic and rooted in greed for Indian land. AIM wanted the public to change its racial bias against Indians, who usually are perceived (and portrayed by the media) in negative ways. Their leaders were angered by "the trail of broken treaties," which is what they call the U.S. government's long history of arbitrary disregard for terms to which it had agreed. AIM wanted Indian culture to be preserved and integrated with their children's education for modern life. They wanted an end to fragmentation of Indian families caused by sending children miles away to schools that alienate them from their own traditions, thereby creating situations ripe for internecine strife. Essentially, they wanted social and economic justice.

AIM was founded in 1968. When its leaders became convinced that peaceful demonstrations and appeals through channels had negligible effect, they started experimenting more frequently with organized, symbolic violence that was intended to draw extensive media coverage. Just before the 1972 presidential election, AIM occupied the Bureau of Indian Affairs building in Washington, D.C., where they caused $2 million in damage and from which they stole BIA files to prove government abuse of Indians. These were made available to the media and became the basis of a widely read newspaper story that gave them headlines, the public's sympathy, congressional inquests, and the allocation of more money for Indian affairs. The gains were slight but they were measureable.

At Wounded Knee, AIM again made it clear that it had learned much from TV's portrayal of street politics in the 1960s, when McLuhan's medium cool hotted up many groups that had previously been shut out of the institutionalized political process because they had been lulled into passivity through the combined forces of suppression and neglect.

Minorities who did not understand political power learned how to get government attention by watching their own or the community's television as blacks ransacked the nation's big cities, and as demonstrators at the 1968 Democratic Convention chanted triumphantly, in the face of police brutality: "The whole world's watching! The whole world's watching!" Television is both educator and democratizer; it personalizes oppression in a way that print and radio do not; it spans great distances, allowing isolated people to feel a sense of community among themselves and with others whose problems are similar. Minorities could see that it terrifies government officials into actually doing something about grievances. AIM drew the obvious conclusion: access to power could be had through television.

Undoubtedly, Wounded Knee was a media event, cleverly staged to spotlight the Indian's lack of civil rights. This is evidenced by the fact that AIM leaders phoned the TV stations and wire services as soon as their command of the hamlet was secure. But, in a certain sense, their action was no more staged than presidential press conferences that are designed to make the chief executive look good.

Wounded Knee's publicity was a massive success for the Indians. 200 activists were soon outnumbered by 300 federal marshals, FBI agents, and a small army of journalists representing several countries (nearly 200, at one point). This time the whole world *was* watching. For ten weeks Indians held the public's attention, via the press, even though the government barred reporters from Wounded Knee after the first month, and the Watergate investigation began competing for time, space, and audiences. The activists had a keen understanding of TV's fascination with dramatic imagery, particularly simple, powerful symbols: Indian dress, negotiations with government officials in a tepee, medicine men, war paint, peace pipes, and the chanting of Sioux invocations for bravery. The press was courted, through background information and interviews, most of which did not find its way onto the nightly TV news, whose format reduces complex events to brief time slots that can be as short as 30 seconds, but they did get some coverage almost every evening during the occupation.

AIM was not alone in being media conscious, or in learning from previous TV news programs. The Justice Department was also a student of television. Therefore, the government decided there were to be no pictures of a marshal's smoking gun held over the body of a dead Indian. That kind of imagery, from Vietnam's livingroom war, had done much damage to government credibility, and there were to be no repeat performances of it on American soil. Despite exchanges of gunfire, which were heavy at times, the Nixon administration's basic strategy was to wait it out. Their decision was reinforced by polling organizations, whose samplings showed that most people sympathized with the Indians. And so the vast array of military hardware that rimmed Wounded Knee was held in check, while phantom jets made periodic reconnaissance flights over the hamlet.

Nixon's administration framed its Wounded Knee policy with the media in mind. This was a realist's approach because every government move was scrutinized by reporters. Their problem was delicate, not only because President Nixon had come into office on a law-and-order platform and the takeover defied established authority, but because congressional politicans wanted a quick resolution of the conflict without undue force, but also without the government yielding to the insurgents. Since the Indians had public support, the government could not use its considerable power without risking a replication of the Wounded Knee Massacre. Furthermore, officials had to keep in mind that Indians everywhere were following events at Wounded Knee via TV (as were other disadvantaged minorities). They, too, might want to oust their tribal councils as mere puppets of the U.S. government. AIM's rebellious fever might become contagious. It would hardly do for a handful of militants to carry out a successful insurrection against the federal government with the whole drama shown on television, home and abroad. Administration officials therefore decided on a policy of containment: the best approach was to let AIM bore the American public to death with their demands, their rituals, their intransigence in the face of an apparently accommodating, patient, benevolent government.

Elsewhere there were rebellious outbursts in sympathetic response to Wounded Knee, and this again negates McLuhan's medium cool theory. Indians went on a rampage in Lumberton, North Carolina, and kidnapped a mayor in New Mexico. Ralph Abernathy, president of the Southern Christian Leadership Conference, expressed his solidarity on CBS in response to AIM's televised appeal for help: ". . . I realized today that Black people will never be free in this nation until our red Indian brothers and sisters are free." ("CBS Morning News" transcript, March 8, 1973) From the government's point of view, it must have been ominous to see a black leader, whose people comprise 11 percent of the population, use television to establish a community of interest with several hundred thousand Indians who had never been organized, and therefore were weak politically.

As time passed, other non-Indian activists began drifting toward Wounded Knee. When the winter's first blizzard arrived in South Dakota, convoys of supplies started moving out from various parts of the United States. One group of Californians was arrested as soon as they crossed state lines. The FBI charged them with aiding and abetting rioters through the interstate shipment of food, medicine, and clothing (no weapons). This strategy was part of a systematic, nationwide crackdown on Indians and their sympathizers who tried to reach

Wounded Knee with help. One key objective of the Justice Department's overall policy was to settle the takeover before summer vacation, otherwise college students might respond to media coverage by swelling the ranks of activists in South Dakota, or by inciting demonstrations elsewhere.

Understandably, the Nixon administration wanted to manipulate the media, as most administrations have wanted to from time to time, but they particularly wanted to influence television, with its nationwide audience, because its news seemed to favor the Indians. The problem was, how to go about it? There is an adversary relationship between government and the press in the United States, which means public officials cannot order journalists to do what they want them to do. The government may request or suggest, it may plead that something be reported or deleted in the national interest, but broadcasting is not an official arm of government, as it is in some countries, and having its view of events presented on TV is not always easy. In the case of Wounded Knee, two weeks after the takeover, CBS's Eric Sevareid, reporting from Washington D.C., broadcast a strong progovernment editorial that was incorporated into Walter Cronkite's evening news program. The essence of his message was:

> The siege of Wounded Knee has become a dangerous, unpredictable struggle . . . on one side the young Indian militants [are] practicing the politics of hysteria, including hatred, romanticism, the instinct for martyrdom. They use weapons of the weak, which are powerful in an underdog-conscious democracy. Here in Washington officials concerned are nervous, divided in their advice, desperately anxious to avoid a pitched battle, uncertain as to how long they can just wait it out. . . . More militants have entered the siege area, which cannot be sealed completely without far greater forces. More weapons have gone in. Reports continue of militant stirrings in some other reservations. Just waiting it out may make a final resolution much harder. . . . The young militants now in charge at Wounded Knee pretty clearly want a battle. . . . The conviction among officials here is that the Indian militants don't want serious negotiations, that every concession will merely mean bigger demands. . . . The watchword here is restraint, in furtherance of which higher level officials of demonstrated coolness are going to the scene. But the militants are talking wilder . . . and the federal forces on their twelve-hour shifts are getting wearier. An irretrievable incident is always possible . . . ("CBS Evening News with Walter Cronkite," March 12, 1973)

Cronkite's name added prestige and legitimacy to the editorial. His program was the perfect vehicle for reaching the largest TV news audience. The day after this editorial, the administration decided to cut off supplies to Wounded Knee (an order that was later rescinded) and announced that ". . . our policy is going to be much more severe this time than it has been before," whereupon a new barricade was erected quickly and armored personnel carriers, heavy trucks, and helicopters were mobilized. However, no attack ensued.

It has been alleged by one of the government's key decision makers of Wounded Knee policy that the Sevareid editorial was not a coincidence. Allegedly, the government asked someone with good connections in broadcasting circles, who also was sympathetic to the Nixon administration, to arrange for the government's views to be telecast, and that Sevareid's editorial was the result of that effort. Richard Salant, who was president of CBS news at the time, is firm in his contradiction of this allegation. In a letter to the author, Salant says:

> If you, or your informant, are charging that Eric Sevareid's commentary of March 12, 1973 was due to any pressure of any kind, you are utterly mistaken. Eric Sevareid is not that kind of person, and CBS News is not that kind of organization. . . .
> I cannot state with certainty whether "a government representative asked CBS to broadcast something on its Evening News, in 1973, that would support the administration's approach and policy at Wounded Knee. . . ." As you must realize, representations are constantly made to us—by the government, by business organizations, by groups and individuals interested in one cause or another—urging us to do a favorable story about them. This may, if the matter is newsworthy, provide a lead for us, but we never—and I repeat, never—roll over and do such a story without full research and checking all sides. . . . We do not serve, we never have served, and we never will serve as a conduit or an amplifying system for *any* viewpoint—including the government's.*

Negotiations between Indians and the government dragged on through April. On May 1 CBS invited M. Stanton Evans, editor of the *Indianapolis News,* to give his opinion about Wounded Knee on their morning news. It was another proadministration editorial, castigating the activists:

> The performance of the Federal Government towards the Indian militants . . . has been a masterpiece of liberal vacillation . . . the collection of troublemakers, ex-cons and convicted felons masquerading as Indian leaders . . . For some reason the liberal commentators, fawning over the so-called American Indian Movement don't tell us that AIM leader Dennis Banks has been convicted of charges including assault, battery and burglary or that the two Bellecourt brothers have both been convicted of burglary and armed robbery. . . .

If criminal acts were relevant in analyzing the significance of Wounded Knee, then Evans, or one of the CBS reporters, could have brought out that government officials often used theft, bribery, murder, and a long list of unconstitutional acts in order to take Indian lands. In so doing, the federal government tolerated practices that have been compared with genocide. The

---

*The complete text of Mr. Salant's letter appears at the end of this chapter.

difference between the Bellecourts's and Banks's misdeeds, when compared with those of government officials, is that the Indians spent time in jail for them whereas federally employed criminals seldom were brought to justice.

For several months after the Wounded Knee settlement on May 8, there were heated debates as to whether or not the media had been used to create the news. Of course it was used. AIM planned the takeover as a media event. Its leaders wanted and got extensive publicity. But the Indians also were used by the media, for AIM had chosen well with respect to location and symbolism. The Indians played their parts with skill and their cause roused public interest as well as sympathy. What could be more appealing in a land of equality than for a small, oppressed minority to beg for justice under the law and to ask for human rights? Wounded Knee was good copy. It helped to boost newspaper circulation and TV news audiences, neither of which hurt profits or prestige. The media and the Indians were silent partners, working together on the same scenario, but without overt collaboration. Each knew precisely what the other was doing. Of the three groups, it was the administration that had nothing to gain. The government was embarrassed by worldwide publicity about its present and past mistreatment of the Indians. Yet it could not use overwhelming force to quell the insurrection because the press constrains abusive authority, and the use of undue power could subvert government credibility.

American Indians have not been oppressed because they are a small minority of several hundred thousand in a country of more than 220 million. They have been oppressed because the government ignored their peaceful pleas for better treatment and justice. This lack of responsiveness taught the Indians that they would not have wrongs redressed unless they resorted to violence, because that is a proven method for attracting official attention and, possibly, public sympathy. Previous television coverage of protests gave the Indians lessons in strategy and tactics, including how the medium can be used to communicate between and among hostile forces. When the government announced that it might take harsher measures to deal with the activists, it was talking not only to TV news audiences, but also to AIM leaders inside of Wounded Knee. Both sides tried to manipulate the media to woo public opinion because leaders cannot accomplish much without the consent of the governed if a society is truly democratic. Because the United States has a free press, the government's authority was checked tightly. One misstep and it would have been reported instantly, with negative effects on authority, civic order, national community, and government credibility.

Wounded Knee clearly illustrated that television is not always a medium to cool passions, even if it does require viewers to fill in its low definition (sketchy information, closely cropped visuals) with their imagination. Television is sometimes hot and sometimes cool, depending on events and their context. The street politics of the 1960s documented this. There are times when TV will hot up a situation, and there are times when it may be used as a cooling agent. Some social critics believe the Watts, California riots would not have occurred if blacks had had access to TV before the violence started. More investigative reporting by television journalists might help to relieve societal pressures if they are discussed openly on the public's airwaves.

THE 1968 DEMOCRATIC NATIONAL CONVENTION

A dramatic example of television as a hot medium is the 1968 Democratic National Convention in Chicago, where one of the last old-time political bosses, Mayor Richard Daley, ruled as if by divine right. The Republican presidential candidate that year, Richard M. Nixon, had already been nominated on a law-and-order platform. When demonstrations against the war in Indochina escalated into riots outside of Convention Hall, they seemed to prove Nixon's contention that disorder endangered the country.

Relatively few viewers in 1968 analyzed the social, political, and psychological effects of televising Mayor Daley's police squads brutalizing rioters. But the Democratic presidential hopefuls, who were at the convention, analyzed them as they watched the televised chaos with mounting dismay. They knew it made their party look incompetent and weak. Also, they were outraged to see police roughing up students as if they were hardened criminals. It was reported that Republican Party leaders watched, too, and rejoiced at the televised property damage and disregard for public authority because it made candidate Nixon look like a timely savior.

That TV was an important means of communication within Convention Hall as well as in the city itself is an interesting political phenomenon. Because of a Chicago telephone strike, communicaton was a bizarre combination of twentieth-century electronics and foot messengers who ran or bicycled information back and forth. That was sometimes more reliable than sending messages by car, because Mayor Daley enforced strict parking regulations for journalists as well as the public. In addition, throngs of demonstrators had taken over the streets, so cars were not as useful as they might have been in compensating for the telephone strike. Delegates and party leaders relied on TV sets to tell them what was happening outside. Within Convention Hall, where crowds made it difficult to move and hear, it was easier to follow speeches and keep abreast of the riots by watching TV.

Chicago was one of those instances where the medium itself hotted up the action it covered. Rioters played up to the cameras and TV crews seemed to encourage them, possibly because police brutality angered the journalists who were as unable to stop it as anyone else. An additional complication is that TV misled viewers into thinking the situation was worse than it was. NBC broadcast certain violent scenes twice, from different angles, without advising viewers that they were seeing a rerun instead of new action. For example, on August 28 at

8:45 p.m., NBC showed the action along Balboa and Michigan Avenues. Curb-to-curb protesters moved like a relentless lava flow, screaming at police, "Hell no! We won't go!" (The televised lesson of Watts was not lost on these demonstrators. Three years previously black activists had set that city aflame to protest social and political injustice. When TV cameras arrived, the blacks knew a national audience was watching as they fueled fires, shouting with glee, "Burn, baby! Burn!") The cameras focused on Michigan Avenue as antiwar protesters belligerently refused to obey police orders. When officers retaliated with macing, clubbing, and arresting innocent bystanders along with demonstrators, the chant changed from "Hell, no! We won't go!" to "The whole world's watching! The whole world's watching!" This scene was followed by a switch back to NBC's anchormen inside Convention Hall. At 9:50 p.m., about an hour later, the screen again was covered with rioters and embattled police along Balboa and Michigan. For the second time viewers saw the same woman, in a striped dress at the same location, going through the same movements, except that this time she was seen from the front. Probably two cameras were shooting from different angles and the footage from both had been used. Similary, a bearded man wearing a plaid shirt was arrested from the left side of the screen at 8:45 p.m. Later, he was "arrested" again, but that camera angle was from the front. Nothing was said to the viewing audience about these repeats. The NBC voiceover simply referred to a "continuing war" in Chicago. The inflammatory rhetoric and unlabeled duplicate images exacerbated rather than cooled the situation.

Considering the utter chaos that ensued from Mayor Daley's lack of cooperation with the press, the intensity of violence in the streets, and the telephone strike, a case can be made that NBC did not realize it rebroadcast the same coverage from different angles. However, the point is that McLuhan's theory of television as a medium cool did not hold on this occasion. Chicago demonstrators gave video lessons in rioting to other viewers who would use similar tactics for future confrontations with authorities.

One spillover effect of being hot history's electronic scribe is that television enhanced its own authority. As traditional idols fell before the camera's eye, images of destruction became the new icons. Society polarized between those who wanted a return to law and order and those who wanted to upend the Establishment's military-industrial complex with the aid of TV journalism. Television became the medium of truth because "seeing is believing."

APPENDIX: 2/28/79 Letter from
Richard Salant to Dr. Saldich

February 28, 1979

Dear Dr. Saldich:

I am not clear how far your allegation reaches. If it charges, or implies, that any stories we did about Wounded Knee or any other subject, or the treatment of those stories, were at the behest of the Federal government, or in response to any pressure by anyone in the Federal government, my denial is certain and flat. CBS News, which has long prided itself on its independence—from government pressures, from business pressures, from organizational pressures, or from anybody else—does not respond to such pressures, and I challenge you to establish a single incident of our having done so.

If you, or your informant, are charging that Eric Sevareid's commentary of March 12, 1973 was due to any pressure of any kind, you are utterly mistaken. Eric Sevareid is not that kind of person, and CBS News is not that kind of organization.

As for Stanton Evans' "pro-administration statement" on the CBS Morning News of March 1, 1973, I would first point out that Mr. Evans is not a CBS staff correspondent, reporter, or commentator, but is an independent on-the-air participant in our Spectrum series. Their work on Spectrum is the equivalent of independent columnists' Op-Ed. pieces for newspapers. They choose whatever topics they wish and treat them in any way they wish without consultation with CBS News. I am certain that Mr. Evans, whom I know to be a man of firm views and integrity, did his piece entirely independently. It would be impossible for his piece to have been "the result of a discussion between CBS and the government" since CBS does not participate, as I have noted, in the topics chosen by the Spectrum participants or in their treatment of those topics.

I cannot state with certainty whether "a government representative asked CBS to broadcast something on its Evening News, in 1973, that would support the administration's approach and policy at Wounded Knee. . . ." As you must realize, representations are constantly made to us—by the government, by business organizations, by groups and individuals interested in one cause or another—urging us to do a favorable story about them. This may, if the matter is newsworthy, provide a lead for us, but we never—and I repeat, never—roll over and do such a story without full research and checking all sides. And when we do a story like Wounded Knee, we, as any professional news organization, seek out the news of all the contending sides. But our position with the government especially is one which ought to be, as it is with all good news organizations, what has been described by commentators as "adversary." We do not serve, we never have served, and we never will serve as a conduit or an amplifying system for *any* viewpoint—including the government's.

At this late date—six years after the alleged episode—I see no purpose in conducting an investigation on whether "a government representative ask[ed] CBS to have someone broadcast their view of Wounded Knee," and there is no practical way to do so. Over one thousand people comprise CBS News, and a number of them who were here in 1973 are no longer here. How do I check? I refuse, on the basis of your blind allegation, to send out 1000 questionnaires or demand affidavits. If, however, your source is willing to disclose to you, and you are willing to disclose to me, with whom your source alleges he made his/her representations, I will pursue it further. If not, I must let it rest.

I would note with dismay that your manuscript is already in the hands of the publisher, and all you are willing to do is to assure me that if your "source is wrong, I would like to include your denial." Surely good scholarship as well as good journalism would require you to have presented this matter to us before the manuscript is completed and has gone to the publisher. Surely if your source is wrong, something more than an inclusion of our denial would be in order.

I find this charge ironic in any event, since what criticism we were subjected to for our coverage of Wounded Knee was that we were too favorable to the Indians, not to the government.

Yours sincerely,

2

HOW TV GOVERNS

AN OVERVIEW

Throughout the modern world, television has altered patterns of governing as well as participation in the political process. This is seen most clearly in countries where radio and TV are used as instruments of power without apology to anyone. It is also seen in the United States where television not only influences but now also exercises certain governmental functions.

TV executives are key political gatekeepers. They regulate access to a majority of the body politic, our vast viewing public. Because they decide what that public will know, they control an important, daily political agenda that influences government priorities and profoundly affects the nation's morale. Broadcasters also have reshaped our elective process to accommodate television's technology and time constraints. This has weakened the party system, diminished convention politics, and raised election costs to exorbitant heights while expanding television's role in governing America.

Paralleling its intrusion on government, television has been and continues to be a great democratizer. It is a corridor to power for those outside the system who are usually ignored or oppressed: minorities, women, senior citizens, children, the infirm, and imprisoned. For these neglected people, TV offers a means of mobilizing public opinion to pressure authorities for a serious hearing of grievances, which might result in social or political justice. Critics may argue that broadcasters were browbeaten into every bit of public service they provided and that benefits resulting from televised events are accidental, not intentional. This is an old debate with compelling arguments on both sides. Whatever the motives, TV's track record shows that it has proliferated and revitalized democratic values more effectively than any other societal force.

Essentially, the problem of electronic democracy is power. Our government was designed so that power is automatically checked and balanced to avoid tyranny. For added good measure the Constitution guarantees a free press, which took on the self-appointed task of holding government accountable to the people. That press has grown from penny sheets to powerful institutions during these past two centuries. It, too, is subject to corruption unless its political power is checked and balanced. But how should this be done? By the television industry itself? By government? By press councils? By citizens' groups? By use of television archives? By teaching electronic literacy? By technological innovation? By a combination of these?

All power ultimately rests on belief. Since TV is used and believed more than any other information source, its impact on American democracy is enormous. How does television affect authority, order, community, and credibility in the government? These are the pivots on which this discussion turns.

THE DYNAMICS

Television's political power has no equal in government, big business, religion, education, or among pressure groups. While some sectors of society may spend more time, money, and talent promoting their particular interests, none has instant, simultaneous televised access to the national body politic. Control of that access is a distinctively political function called gatekeeping. This privilege of broadcasters, who are neither elected nor appointed to public office, gives them more raw power than any of the people's representatives. Even presidents must obtain their permission for access although, legally, the airwaves belong to the public.

Regulating access gives broadcasters important leverage not only in day-to-day government. This leverage is intensified particularly during elections because many campaigners believe TV is the most effective medium for reaching their constituents. Unlike some countries where candidates are legally entitled to free and equal air time, our candidates must compete with advertisers to buy time, as if political and product information were equally important to the public good. Time is sold at the discretion of station managers, who can and do refuse to sell it. Politicians try to stay on good terms with them, not only during campaigns but also while they are in office. After all, there is always the next election to consider. Pleasing these gatekeepers naturally results in self-censorship by politicians. Although they may resent or dislike the electronic press, most of them conform to TV's demands, court its favor and, as a result, they enlarge broadcasters' governmental functions.

Television's power is enhanced further by its penchant for hiring former government officials. TV stations are everywhere and so are the opportunities. For instance, although President Nixon was forced to resign in national disgrace, he earned a small fortune as the star in David Frost's televised interviews. President Jimmy Carter's former budget director, Bert Lance, was drummed out of office for alleged conflict of interest. Some say he was persecuted by journalists, but Lance was careful not to alienate the press during his nationally televised hearings. Those weeks before the camera's eye, under hot lights and tough questioning, prepared him well for his new career as a highly paid TV commentator in his home state of Georgia. Richard E. Wiley was once head of the Federal Communications Commission (FCC), which regulates TV. On retirement he became an unsalaried board member of the Television and Radio Political Action Committee, one of the nation's most powerful lobbies. Obviously, his extensive contacts in Washington and his inside knowledge of government regulatory procedures is invaluable to broadcasting, just as the industry's continuing need for legal counsel is invaluable to Wiley's law firm.

Though a symptom of serious illness, this revolving door syndrome pales to insignificance when compared with another problem for American democracy: television is the sole source of information about public affairs for millions of people, many of whom think it is objective because they believe what they see. It is natural to think that if we see something we know what happened, or even understand it. But any criminal lawyer could cite many cases where several eyewitnesses of the same event "saw" different things. Nonetheless, many people hold fast to old cliches: "Seeing is believing," "The camera never lies." Unwittingly, sole-users produce a situation similar to censorship because they give themselves only one version of events, the televersion.

Historically, political and spiritual leaders decided what the people would know and when they would know it. Now it is broadcasters who exercise this leadership role for a majority of the public. Until print was invented in the fifteenth century, there was a direct ratio between ignorance of the masses and their obedience. Knowledge is the fuel of civic disorder. Before printing enlarged and quickened the circulation of news, large-scale rebellions were rare. With the Age of Enlightenment, knowledge was no longer the preserve of a privileged few, but rulers controlled printing's subversive potential by licensing printers in order to censor their work.

Broadcasters dredge up the historic relationship between licensing and censorship when they wish to paint themselves as oppressed journalists engaged in a struggle for freedom of the press against government's infringement on their First Amendment rights. It is an appealing but inaccurate self-portrait. TV executives do not admit to differences between then and now, or between print and the electronic press. Freedom of content, which was severely curtailed by royal licenses, is the rule not the exception in television. It is specifically guaranteed by federal regulation.

Unlike print, the number of electronic "newspapers" is necessarily restricted by space available on the broadcast spectrum, which is always less than demand. Would-be competitors cannot set up their own station at will, even with all the money in hand that would be necessary for such an enterprise. This means that stations get a monopoly when they receive a license because no other station can occupy that segment of the spectrum once it is assigned. Eventually the problem of scarcity will disappear. Technological progress in video communication by cable, satellite, microwave relay, fiber optics, and lasers will provide a multitude of channels from which to choose: predictions range widely, from hundreds to thousands. Once such a competitive force is available, reasonable access to video audiences by a diversity of interests may be a reality. When that happens there may be no compelling reason for government licensing.

Because competition is limited by the number of stations that can fit on the broadcast spectrum, TV executives charge advertisers whatever the traffic will bear. And it bears a lot. The record shows that with few exceptions, TV ads increase product sales dramatically. Therefore air time is sold at incredible rates. A charge of $100,000 a minute for prime time is not uncommon. One-shot spectaculars, such as the 1978 Superbowl game, brought $325,000 a minute. If broadcasters are suffering from governmental persecution, it is well hidden among consistently high earnings that have not slumped during depressions or major recessions when other sectors of the economy were under great stress. TV can charge extravagant prices for its advertising because it is so much more powerful than print. It is the medium's extraordinary power that causes some people to argue that the First Amendment does not apply to TV in the same way that it applies to newspapers.

A UNIQUE POLITICAL POWER

Television derives its distinctive powers from instant, simultaneous access to an immense audience, high credibility, and the fact that it is our only national newspaper other than the *Wall Street Journal*, whose audience is specialized. The commercial networks' nightly news reaches nearly 55 million people. Newspapers, no matter how good they are, do not even begin to have that kind of readership. For them, 1 million would be a sizable circulation. Advertisers spend fortunes for air time because they want, and get, access to an audience that runs in the tens of millions.

Even if a newspaper is read by 1 million people, it is read at various times rather than simultaneously, and much of it is skipped completely or skimmed quickly. Television is a more intense information experience. It is a continuum that cannot be scanned. Viewers cannot turn to the next frame, glancing at or ignoring an ad or a news item, picking and choosing as they please. Choice does not exist within a TV program. Viewers are a captive audience. The medium, not the person, is in control. The machine dominates users' information-consuming behavior, rendering them passive recipients of what someone else has decided they should know and when they should know it.

The political implications of this power to manipulate are beyond measure. Imagine a national emergency such as war, or a major earthquake. It would be easier and more effective to broadcast orders than to publish them. A newspaper would not reach as many people, or be read simultaneously. It might be skimmed and important information missed. The power of command that broadcasting has is superior to print because television's high credibility is the envy of every other medium and of many authority structures in the United States. Let us take an example from radio broadcasts. During the Algerian War, President Charles de Gaulle communicated by radio with loyalist troops on Algerian territory. Portable transistor radios made it possible for soldiers, even in remote districts, to disobey local officers and follow de Gaulle's orders which he broadcast from Paris. Many of them did. If we apply this example to television, we can deduce that there would be similar cooperation. Imagine the force of an order, or a strong suggestion, if it were issued on TV by a nationally respected person such as CBS's Walter Cronkite, or even by that much-loved TV personality, Archie Bunker. Print cannot duplicate that kind of power because it does not have television's immense audience, its instant and simultaneous access, its high credibility, or its nationwide scope. That is why there is no meaningful comparison between print and TV. Print is important in its own sphere, and it provides a valuable antidote to the superficial nature of televised information. But the two modes of communication are distinctively, irrevocably different.

TV AND THE FIRST AMENDMENT: GOVERNMENT REGULATION

Broadcasters use the public's airwaves at no cost to themselves. Ironically, it is consumers (not just viewers) who pay for them to have this privilege. The system is really quite simple. Manufacturers raise the price of their TV-advertised goods to meet the medium's expensive rates, which are the source of broadcasters' steady and enormous profits. In that way commercial networks use the public's airwaves at no cost, manufacturers advertise at no cost, and the public finances the arrangement. It is an undeclared system of pay-TV, or, in political terms, of taxation without representation.

One might think that television executives would be eager to express gratitude for this free ride by providing public service programming. The record shows that they are not. Broadcasters have done little in the way of public service programming except when they were compelled or when they used it as a guise to increase their power. This is fact, not criticism. Human selfishness is an underlying assumption of our Constitution. America's Founding Fathers knew that they had to harness it to the public good so that people would work on behalf of the commonweal while gaining something for themselves. This is how they forged a sense of national community out of 13 jealous, competitive, independent states. The method has its flaws but it has worked effectively for almost 200 years. Therefore, it is in our democratic tradition for TV to be profit motivated and for a federal regulatory agency to look after the public's interest. That agency, the Federal Communications Commission, was created by Congress, which gave it quasi-legal power to make binding rules. The FCC's most impressive function is the issuing of broadcast licenses for a three-year term. These can be revoked if stations do not meet vaguely defined public interest needs such as airing programs of concern to the community in which they broadcast. It is the station's responsibility to determine those needs during regular ascertainment periods. This is done in a variety of ways, such as surveying community leaders or soliciting viewers' opinions. Because the industry is not public-service oriented it would be a grievous policy error to rescind these relatively mild constraints, unless they are replaced by some other mechanism that obliges the networks to operate in the public's interests.

Because the FCC almost never revokes a TV license, some people think the Commission has succumbed to the television industry's vast political power and that it works hand in glove with broadcasters to maintain the status quo. This view of the FCC can be documented to a impressive degree, but it is not shared by television executives who fear the Commission's licensing power and regard it as a means for harassing their industry. Therefore, broadcasters argue that FCC rules infringe the Constitution's First Amendment protection of journalists which they cite tirelessly, while hoping that no one will notice they are predominantly an entertainment medium and that TV is a part of the press only in a peripheral, not an essential, way. Said differently, one could argue that it has no right to First Amendment protection. Admittedly, this is a heady bit of logic, but the ambiguity is suggested by CBS's "Evening News with Walter Cronkite." Beginning with the April 16, 1973 broadcast of this program, CBS applied for a copyright, claiming not that its news is a legitimate journalistic activity but that it is "an unpublished motion picture other than a photoplay." On this ground the copyright was granted!

When the First Amendment is taken out of context, as is often done by broadcasters, nothing could be more simple: "Congress shall make no law abridging the freedom of speech, or of the press. . . ." Obviously this means that the government, including the legislative branch, has no constitutional right to regulate television with rules that have the force of law. And FCC rules do have the force of law because they are binding. However, if the First Amendment is not taken out of context, if we bear in mind that the overall purpose of the Constitution is to separate and divide power so that it cannot become tyrannous, then simplicity gives way to complexity. Then, a strong argument can be made that television has staggering political power, unlike the press that this amendment was intended to protect, which is print journalism.

The point at which the two media can no longer be thought of in the same way is where television passes from reporting and influencing to actually governing. For this reason television's power must be checked and balanced if democracy is to be protected. Naturally this interpretation of the Constitution is not popular among broadcasters. They have consistently lobbied for federal deregulation of their industry.

IMMEDIACY VERSUS CIVIC ORDER

When print dominated communications, the time lag between events and their publication allowed government a grace period to assess and interpret facts. This breathing space between receiving and responding to information was possible because linear knowledge is sequential. There is the event, the reporting, the printing, the circulation itself and, finally, the reading and sharing. This process itself helped to maintain civic order. It also encouraged corruption, which thrives on secrecy. Nevertheless, during crises, delays shore up stability because authorities have time to think things through in order to short-circuit impending panic. Now, however, the electronic press covers many events live, or reports them immediately after they happen, sometimes even before officials know about them. This is one of the ways that broadcasters not only influence but also set the political agenda. The results are that television encroaches on a traditional governmental function, and it contributes to political instability since the press wants everything to be known publicly, now, regardless of how impolitic that may be.

Democracy takes time. Electronic communication values immediacy and is intolerant of reasoned thought. With few notable exceptions, governmental secrecy is hard to come by, not only because there are deliberate leaks to the press but because journalists tend to equate secrecy with wrongdoing. History has often proved them right. However, it is worth remembering that this nation was conceived in secrecy as well as in liberty. The ideas on which American democracy are based were hammered out during a hot, humid Philadelphia summer, behind closed doors, among men who vowed that their discussions would not be made public. One wonders whether the United States would ever have come into being if the Founding Fathers were obliged to give a daily accounting of their progress to accommodate the 7:00 P.M. news feed. In political affairs, timing is crucial. Only after agreement had been reached among themselves did the authors of the Constitution make public its contents and seek its ratification by the people.

A nation's business cannot be done in public all the time. Journalists know this because they know that even their business cannot be done in public all the time. They are aware particularly of the need for secrecy to protect their sources of information and their files. Yet the press behaves as if government can function well only when journalists are present at the birth of policy or have access to information immediately, regardless of whether publicity is in the nation's interest. National interest is a concept behind which governments everywhere hide many grievous misdeeds. Nonetheless, occasionally, "the fence of wisdom *is* silence" and the people's representatives should be allowed to maintain silence without an automatic assumption of guilt.

IMPACT ON LINEAR ILLITERATES

Belief and power are two sides of the same coin. Both are affected greatly by television. This is true particularly for millions of Americans who read and write poorly or not at all. They are our linear illiterates. For them television is important because it requires no formal schooling to be understood superficially!

All TV content has a politicizing effect. The formerly passive are learning about politics whether they tune in to public affairs programs or only to entertainment. Even seemingly apolitical commercials brim over with subtle commentary on the use of power, with emphasis on differences between the haves and have-nots. They give the impression that what is advertised is attainable. All one needs is money. The hidden political message is this: if the economic pie were sliced differently, the have-nots would get better training and more jobs, which would result in higher salaries with which to buy televised products. Once the underprivileged perceive this message, there is a subtle buildup of political resentment and rising expectations.

Radio and television have introduced electronic literacy. People no longer need to read and write in order to know. Dramatic visuals and simplified content give viewers the *feeling* that they are informed. Events are reduced to a low level of comprehension. Words are no longer barriers. Pictures clarify verbal problems. Political and civic leaders are seen and heard. They become friends or enemies whose televised victories and defeats are vicarious experiences, much like football games. Even if one neither votes nor works on behalf of a cause, this once-removed participation is acquired easily and nurtures political awareness. But it is not knowledge. It is too thin.

There are two serious disadvantages to using television as a sole source of information: (1) superficiality of day-to-day news, which makes it an inadequate basis on which to act, and (2) sole-users are unaware of this superficiality. If viewers have trouble reading and writing, they compound linear illiteracy with poor electronic literacy skills because they have not learned to analyze what they see and hear. Unfortunately, if they do read and write well, they are not necessarily better off because most schools do not teach electronic literacy.

Communication systems always have been seedbeds of rebellion because they are vehicles for exchanging ideas, for conveying motives, creating desires, fostering hopes, and expressing disenchantment. That is why print has a long history of censorship. Traditional religious and political leaders kept the masses ignorant for as long as they could so that they would know little, want little, and obey without question. There was always some holy of holies from which the people were excluded because their leaders knew that the dissemination of information stirs up expectations, unrest, demands, action, and the sharing of power.

Electronic information explains much about contemporary American politics. The dramatic decline in voter turnout for recent presidential elections has been interpreted as an expression of apathy. This is a critical problem for democracy, but voter apathy alone does not account for an entire political process. American politics includes intense activity among and on behalf of interest groups such as consumers, women, minorities, the handicapped, children, senior citizens, and prisoners. They comprise the formerly neglected and ignored who have learned how to use television as a platform for making their grievances public. The emergence of street politics in the 1960s indicated considerable vitality, not apathy.

The one-issue politics of the 1970s, where the focus is sharp and narrow, is exactly what television covers well. Displaced homemakers want pay and benefits, homosexuals demonstrate for acceptance, senior citizens rebel against enforced retirement, women and minorities continue their quest for employment equality. All of them get TV coverage.

To sum up, pressure groups have learned to bridge the years between elections with relentless political activity. This is a sign not of apathy but of vigorous citizen participation especially when it is compared with traditional stop-and-go patterns of ballot box politics.

STATE CENSORSHIP

Third world leaders are particularly sensitive to the political power of radio and television. To many of them it is evident that governments should dictate program content as part of nation building and to avoid subversion. Their broadcasts are outright propaganda, in service to the state. If national goals require everyone to work, regardless of socioeconomic position, the government network provides drama, dance, and musicals to glorify manual labor, even though traditional values relegate work to the lower classes. Or, the state may choose to reinforce custom. This is done by the Arabs, who import many TV programs from the West. But Muslim values dominate their society and therefore the imports are censored so that cigarettes and alcohol are not shown as satisfactory solutions to stress. Similarly, in the interest of national community it is not likely that unstable regimes would feature programs celebrating restless individualism.

State censorship is not limited to authoritarian governments. Indira Gandhi, former prime minister of the world's largest democracy, put a stranglehold on freedom of the press throughout India during her last year in office. In South Vietnam, after years of war to establish democracy, U.S.-supported President Nguyen Van Thieu imposed ruthless censorship on the media, closing down newspapers and dealing roughly with reporters who dared to criticize him or his policies. Even in France, until a few years ago, nationalized television was indisputably an instrument of state. Then, as now, nongovernmental radio stations and the print media were free to compete, but television was the government's own voice. Its director was in daily contact with the prime minister and the president of the Republic, or with their representatives. Reforms have granted more independence to French broadcasters, but when push comes to shove, as in the 1978 elections, the government still finds it difficult to relinquish past privileges. Though French law requires equal air time for all valid candidates, during a specified time span, there are many subtle ways by which incumbent candidates can be more equal than others when it comes to TV news coverage.

Here in the United States the electronic press is free from formal government interference with program content except in wartime when, along with other media, it is mobilized for propaganda to inspire patriots and confound the enemy. All administrations since George Washington's have tried, with varying degrees of success, to influence journalists by persuasion or threats, but generally the United States has a free flow of information. This tradition of maintaining independence for journalists may explain why there is so little comment on the extensive governmental powers that the press has accumulated during the television age. Protecting freedom of the press is so instinctive that Americans do not think often of the reverse danger: encroachment by journalists on governmental functions.

POLITICAL TELEVISION

Television's relationship to politics is both obvious and subtle. Election coverage, political speeches, and interviews with officials are among the more obvious facets of that relationship. Some of the subtleties have already been mentioned: gatekeeping, agenda setting, personalizing power, increased campaign costs, being a corridor to power, instant access to the public, national coverage, credibility, and immediacy. While the subtleties are the focus of this book, it is useful simply to categorize TV's political programs.

Campaigns usually come first to mind. They include formal speeches, debates, news coverage, political advertisements, filmed biographies, interviews, and planned press conferences. Most viewers know these are intended to win friends and influence voters.

Congressional hearings were an early success on TV. They came into their own during the 1950s when Senator Joseph McCarthy used his seat in Congress as a platform from which he conducted a fascist-type campaign against communism. During the famous Congressional Army-McCarthy Hearings, the junior senator from Wisconsin revealed himself to the TV audience as a demagogue who arrogantly disregarded the constitutional rights of witnesses. But his star was waning. McCarthy's credibility already had been undermined a month before the hearings started when CBS's Edward R. Murrow and Fred Friendly broadcast a televised portrait of the senator, comprised of filmclips that etched most finely McCarthy's lack of emotional balance, reasonableness, and respect for others. These were run with minimal commentary but maximum effect. To appreciate the courage of Murrow's and Friendly's program one should remember that even President Dwight Eisenhower hesitated to confront McCarthy. His grip on the nation was remarkable, and the CBS program was a courageous piece of TV journalism.

In this instance television executives rightfully are proud of their service to democracy. It was their medium that revealed McCarthyism on a scale and in a manner that no other medium could match. But this is not the whole picture. Many innocent people in television were ruined personally, politically, and economically because broadcasters, along with print journalists, cooperated with McCarthy during his rise to power instead of helping to expose him.

Since the 1950s there have have been other televised congressional hearings, but none compares with the Senate's Select Committee on Watergate, which opened in the spring of 1973. These hearings revealed President Nixon's corruption, provided viewers with a national civics lesson, and reaffirmed democracy as a system that effectively checks and balances power. Other countries may point with pride to the untried rhetoric of their constitution, but American television was a showcase for democracy in action.

Political editorials are usually the privilege of television personnel who offer their interpretation of the day's news. An innovation that has been used recently are viewers who are invited to respond with mini-editorials of their own in the form of "free speech messages." These were conceived by media-activist Phil Jacklin, a California philosophy professor. Though they last only two or three minutes, they partially fill a station's public service obligations since speakers express themselves about things of significance to the community. Feedback also is designed to let viewers have some access. It expresses public opinion, and is usually read into the news format by reporters rather than viewers.

Although the time allocated for public opinion is never enough to discuss a subject adequately, the symbolism of these innovations is powerful: freedom of speech is being interpreted as a right to be heard as well as to speak. Since local news is a trend setter, much the way that political third parties are, the national news programs may adopt this approach once its popularity is established.

News magazines, such as CBS's popular "60 Minutes" or ABC's "20/20," are attempts at in-depth coverage. They are an antidote to the nightly news, which glosses over most events, and are a belated recognition that length, depth, and quality of information are often related.

The evening news on the three commercial networks (ABC, CBS, and NBC) has a total audience that equals the total population of France, which is about 55 million people. Network news is national because most of the stations throughout the country sign on with one of the Big Three as affiliates and take a news feed about national and international events from that network. These programs consist of 22 minutes. They are divided into topical segments, ranging from 30 seconds to several minutes, and are usually bare-bone headlines without benefit of content interpretation, or commentary, as if television journalists believe that facts speak for themselves. The remaining eight minutes of the half hour are sold to advertisers. Stations usually do their own local news.

Only one nightly national news program covers a single event and explores it in depth for a full half hour. This is done by public television's "MacNeil/ Lehrer Report." Since it is noncommercial, their half hour has a full 30 minutes of news.

Presidential press conferences are very much creatures of the chief executive, who schedules, opens, and closes them, and who decides which reporters will ask questions. The White House staff tries to anticipate every possible subject and the president is briefed carefully about appropriate replies and pitfalls. Journalists try to make this more than a ritual by sacrificing their favorite questions to follow up on one put by a colleague if it was not answered satisfactorily. The frequency of press conferences varies with a president's political style, but they have been an important part of the democratic process in most modern administrations.

Presidential trips. Whether it is to Plains, Georgia or Beijing, China, journalists follow and report the president's travels in microscopic detail. Every move, especially a wrong one, is grist for the news. When President Nixon toured China, the public went along via satellite. President Gerald Ford's occasional awkwardness, such as tripping out of a doorway or falling on a ski slope, was recorded for posterity and magnified beyond reason. President Carter's first diplomatic mission abroad, to seven countries in nine days, was the kind of visual montage that suits the medium: every day a famous face and well-known place. Typically, viewers learn little about foreign or domestic policy from these expensive TV extravaganzas. But they could. A slight effort in the direction of historical perspective or analysis of contemporary political life would improve them significantly.

Interviews always have been important to political television, but 1977 was a benchmark year when viewers throughout the world saw Israel's former Prime Minister Golda Meir and Egypt's President Anwar al-Sadat discuss the possibility of Sadat's first visit to Jerusalem if it would advance the cause of peace. Although the visit had been explored previously through diplomatic channels, no one anticipated that an international television program would be the vehicle for probing the idea of an historic diplomatic mission.

Usually political interviews are scheduled for Sunday afternoons, where they draw a relatively limited audience that numbers six or seven million. What is said by national leaders and visiting dignitaries on "Face the Nation," "Meet the Press," "Issues and Answers," and other interview programs is quoted on radio, the evening TV news, and by opinion makers in the print media. Therefore, it is a mistake to judge these programs by ratings alone. TV interviews are sometimes used by officials as trial balloons to test public acceptance of an idea.

Documentaries are an excellent vehicle for televised investigative reporting. They sometimes deal with controversial, even explosive subjects, such as CBS's "The Selling of the Pentagon," which cataloged the government's vast media resources and its various campaigns not only to inform, but also to mislead the public. Sometimes the networks are accused of shying away from controversy because of the equal-time provisions that govern American broadcasting. A successful right-to-reply claim means a loss of air time for the producing network, which means a loss of advertising revenue due to the displacement of a regularly scheduled program. This is a high risk for a sortie into troubled waters. The validity of this criticism is debatable. There has been some drawing back, a reassessing of documentaries in comparison with magazine formats, but they still can be provocative. In the first month of 1979, there were two highly acclaimed documentaries. One dealt with the plight of refugees from Vietnam who make a perilous escape voyage by sea only to find that they are unwelcome in many countries. The second one was a nonsensationalized, intelligent analysis of child abuse.

The audience for documentaries varies with the subject, but generally it hovers around the seven million figure. By commercial TV standards this does not produce a high rating, which explains why documentaries, like interviews, are not assigned better time slots.

Political speeches are televised in their entirety when the president addresses the nation if station managers consider the issues crucial. Otherwise, highlights may be abstracted for the evening news. CBS and NBC affiliates in the San Francisco area chose not to broadcast President Carter's talk about the Panama Canal treaties. Only ABC's affiliate station carried it live.

In 1978 the networks decided to review their policy about presidential access in terms of the equal-time provision, which they would like to eliminate. By applying it rigorously to the president, as the FCC requires them to do for other political candidates they may cause enough annoyance to get it rescinded. A rigid application of the provision would result in TV time being made available to opposition leaders, which is what an incumbant likes to avoid. Presidents have come to expect extensive TV coverage throughout their tenure, which is one reason why they are so difficult to defeat. But broadcasters are aware that Carter's strategy en route to the White House was to campaign two years in advance of the actual election. Networks do not want to be accused of favoring the president by providing access for politicking rather than for reasons of state. This is why the White House aroused zero interest from the networks when its staff inquired about the possibility of President Carter making a July 4 speech to the nation in 1978.

Presidential media experts occasionally explore ways of getting more coverage on the Public Broadcasting Service (PBS). This is a delicate and perhaps dangerous route from the perspective of democracy, unless the televised messages are clearly labeled as government produced. Federal funding is an important part of public television's budget. It would be tempting to make that funding conditional on presidential coverage, especially now that satellite technology has made PBS a national network.

Docudramas have provoked considerable debate. Critics say they distort history, mislead the public, and glamorize sordidness. One highly popular docudrama was a thinly fictionalized account of President Nixon's decline and fall. Despite playing fast and loose with accuracy, this format has an appeal similar to the historical novel, which professional historians generally disdain. It is likely that docudramas will endure for the same reason historical novels do: people like them. In a free society whose orientation is profit making, that incentive is hard to repress.

Political satire is not common in that there is no running series dealing with it. However, some situation comedies and serious dramas occasionally take up a political theme and work it effectively. TV's best-known bigot, Archie Bunker of "All in the Family," did just that with the subject of conscientious objectors who refused to fight in the U.S.-Indochina war. The program was aired while the nation anguished about draft dodgers, deserters, and amnesty. It was a brilliant, witty, penetrating analysis of complex issues. Although viewers were left laughing, they were also left thinking. (The show endorsed amnesty, which is what was eventually offered by the government under certain conditions.)

Daytime news programs are difficult to categorize. They are neither hard news nor magazines, and they certainly are not documentaries. They tend to blend book reviews with celebrity interviews and general chitchat that is intended to entertain as well as inform. Perhaps they are best described as information shows. They have a good following, in terms of daytime viewership and they do provide information about, and occasionally create, trends. Their themes are not strongly political.

Congress in action is the newest category of political television. Its debut was deferred because of disputes over camera control. The commercial networks argued that freedom of the press would be constrained if they did not work the cameras. Congress thought unrestricted filming would lead to eventual manipulation of their representatives because members might play up to the TV audience. While state-level experiences with televised legislative sessions do not bear out this concern (everyone more or less ignores the technology after a time), the Canadian Parliament urged U.S. congressional leaders to follow their example of keeping a tight rein on TV coverage, and that is what Congress did.

PROBLEMS

American television does not meet the needs of a political system whose well-being depends upon an informed citizenry. Most Americans use TV as a news source, and the majority of those viewers rely solely on it for information about public affairs. That may be good news for the commercial networks but it is bad news for democracy. TV disseminates superficial, frequently irrelevant information that is not an appropriate basis for political action.

U.S. televised news and public affairs programs are excellent when compared with TV news in most other countries, particularly along the dimension of freedom from state control, because only a few nations in the world have a free press. American journalists constantly and rightly guard against any subversion of their freedom, but they have not solved the problem of content superficiality or the arrogance of power. TV news derives its prestige largely from its scope rather than its quality. We have no national newspaper, and although radio also broadcasts coast to coast, it cannot compare with TV's combination of sight and sound.

Given the success of public television's nationwide, nightly, in-depth newscast, the "MacNeil/Lehrer Report," and the commercial networks' successful news magazines, one might expect the commercial networks to focus on quality. But ABC, CBS, and NBC move in lockstep, duplicating each other's work and format despite the absence of depth. Commercial network news is so much alike in scope, content, and visuals that one wonders why they use separate reporters, producers, camera crews, and laboratories. This is one time when competition has not had the salutary effects that we often expect from it: diversity and improved quality. For 20 years the networks' main difference has been to vary slightly their highly paid anchorpeople. ABC's anchorman, Harry Reasoner, was earning a modest salary of $250,000 a year when that network's first anchorwoman, Barbara Walters, signed on for $1 million. ABC was also the first to hire a black anchorman. But new faces have not improved substance.

Despite cost and effort, commercial TV news is seldom bold, investigative, imaginative, or perceptive. Much of it is rip-and-read journalism, a simple repetition of the day's newspaper headlines in sonorous tones. Television had a marvelous opportunity in 1978 when New York City's newspapers were on strike for several months. According to critics, instead of exploring the limits of its potential for reporting, TV delivered the same lightweight news that easily could have been culled by any moderately intelligent person from other papers and magazines. Instead of filling the information gap by expanding or deepening its reporting, television plodded along with 30-second reports and five-minute analyses of complex issues. Obviously the medium can do better. This already has been demonstrated by public TV's "MacNeil/Lehrer Report." The limitations are human, not technical. Network news managers are remarkably unimaginative.

Television executives defend themselves by insisting that they give the audience what it wants. Some evidence suggests that they are out of touch with viewers' preferences. This seems impossible since each network has extensive audience research facilities, whose data supposedly are accurate because they are of great importance as sales tools when discussing with potential advertisers what the body count is per program. Nonetheless, a Harris survey (January 1978) indicates that the public wants more and different kinds of news.

This poll was based on a representative sample of 1,533 adults, as well as 86 top editors and news directors and 76 major reporters and writers. Editors and journalist's were asked how interested they thought the public was in several news categories, and the public participants in this poll were asked how interested they were. Actually, the percentage spread between what the public wants and what media professionals think it wants is startling:

Kind of news	Percent of the public that wants it	Percent of editors, journalists, who think public wants it	Percent by which editors, journalists, misjudge the public
National	60	34	−26
Sports	35	75	−40
World affairs	41	5	−36
Local	74	88	+14
Entertainment, art, cultural	29	45	+16
State	27	62	+35

Admittedly, this is a comprehensive survey, not limited to television. But it indicates that TV news is not an exception to the overall pattern.

Top journalists and editors are usually white, male, middle-aged, middle class, and college educated. Perhaps that explains why they are misinformed about the public. Unless they have frequent contact with the aged and infirm, with a wide spectrum of minorities, women, children, the uneducated, unemployed, imprisoned and underutilized people in all socioeconomic levels, as well as with people like themselves, it is understandable that they have wrong impressions of their audience.

Any serious student of television could have deduced that viewers want more and better news simply by looking at audience figures. The 1976 presidential campaign debates between Gerald Ford and Jimmy Carter attracted immense audiences each time, oscillating between 60 and 80 million viewers. After each debate the press evaluated them as dull and not particularly informative. Yet the audience held or increased each time. Similarly, the televised Watergate hearings kept the nation captive. TV sets were carried to offices and, along with transistor radios, were kept on throughout the day. The hearings found an international audience. Foreigners followed the proceedings with the same avidness that Americans did. Gavel-to-gavel coverage was repeated at night by the Public Broadcasting Service and many people went to work sleepy-eyed the next day from having stayed up to the wee hours of the morning to watch it. Daytime Nielsen ratings compared favorably with the soaps despite hours of tedious testimony and minute cross-examination about seemingly inconsequential details. Another indicator that the public wants more and better news is the fact that nearly 55 million people comprise the commercial networks' nightly news audience, Monday through Friday.* Even presidential speeches attract higher numbers. Figures do go down dramatically for documentaries and interviews but among their viewers are the nation's decision makers, opinion leaders, and students. As agents of socioeconomic and political change, they are a significant minority.

TV is a relatively young medium still exploring its potential. The industry is learning more about its viewers and viewers are learning to articulate their preferences. Increased understanding between the two may yet result in TV news that meets democracy's need for quality information about public affairs.

RESHAPING THE POLITICAL PROCESS

Along with governing and influencing public policy, broadcasters have reshaped the political process itself. They have done this by increasing political participation, personalizing power, making democracy more expensive, hindering reasoned discussion, influencing West Coast voting, weakening parties and conventions, prolonging campaigns, and discouraging public service.

TV Increases Political Participation

During the 1960s and early 1970s, television gave ordinary people access to power. That was the era of media politics and activists who organized those public demonstrations that used techniques particularly compatible with television's voracious appetite for visuals. They were symbolic, dramatic, action-packed, provided new information, and had a potential for erupting into violence.

Broadcasters knew from entertainment programs that violence attracts large audiences. Activists knew it also. In the early years street politicians

---

*Various methods are used to calculate news viewership for the three networks. This figure represents audience per minute during the season (September-February). An average weekly

provoked authorities deliberately, with predictable results: peaceful demonstrations escalated into riots. Television showed a new America, one that was not described in U.S. history books: brutality against college students, white adults jeering and spitting at well-mannered black children as they walked to newly integrated schools, police dogs and cattle prods being used to control black demonstrators, blacks setting fire to and looting cities across the nation, authorities helpless to stop it and confused about how to restore order. The public was outraged to see dead and wounded American soldiers being carried from Indochinese battle zones in a war whose purpose was unclear to many viewers.

TV executives increasingly became aware of how activists used them and their medium, but they were in a quandary because street politics was a trade-off; defiance of authority, with overtones of possible mayhem, increased news audiences. But it also legitimized the politics of violence. Network coverage gave activists extraordinary power by personalizing issues, giving protestors national recognition and building a sense of national community among separated groups, who learned the techniques of organization and civil disobedience from TV.

Paradoxically, although government has become increasingly complex and technical, television has demonstrated time and again that people do make a difference: they can effect change. This has a beneficial effect on democracy as a whole, and it probably will increase as diverse technology affords more and better video access for a wider spectrum of people.

TV Personalizes Power

Personalized power has been with us during the television age to such an extent that we do not think of it as a new phenomenon. To young people it must seem incredible that democracy in America survived for 170 years with only photographs or sketches of civic leaders who, for most of that time, could not talk directly to constituents except in person. During that epoch journalists had considerable political power in that they were the filters through which most news passed. It was they who sorted out what the public should know about official policy. Candidates and office holders were relieved when radio came along, for it gave them direct access to voters when broadcasters let them use it. Radio proved its effectiveness during World War II. Hitler, Churchill, de Gaulle, and Roosevelt were master orators who comforted and rallied their people over the air.

Presidential power has increased dramatically since television began covering politics. Congressional power went into comparative decline until the televised Watergate hearings when it regained prestige as an effective check on the executive branch of government. It is natural that television focused on the presidency because the medium does well when there is simplicity. It is easier to

audience would approximate 80 million viewers. *Source*: Telephone interview with Nancy Mead, NBC Audience Measurement Department, July 13, 1979.

deal with a single personality than with several hundred congressional representatives. One spillover effect of presidential television is the chief executive's tendency to circumvent Congress by going directly to the people. President de Gaulle did this with great skill. He had little respect for the National Assembly and he commandeered television regularly in order to build up his own national constituency among the people.

Another aspect of TV's personalized power is that the public is also being seen and heard. Initially they were part of the news coverage, especially during the era of street politics. As interest groups gained power, their representatives· were interviewed in their own right as opinion leaders.

Technology seems to be pulling society in two directions. On the one hand, life has become so sophisticated that much of it is beyond comprehension: only a relatively small segment of society understands technology and science, much less their policy implications and general effect on human development. On the other hand, technology is becoming simplified and miniaturized. Ten years ago a room-sized computer was needed for certain computations that can now be done with a silicon chip that is smaller than a thumbnail. TV photography used to be the province of specialists who needed a crew of people to lug around massive equipment. Technological innovations have introduced film that works well in the dimmest light; many cameras are automatic so that people who think of themselves as technically inept can produce fine pictures; miniaturization has given us easily carried equipment that provides more diversity of coverage by a wider spectrum of people.

The personalizing process is a spillover effect of advanced science and technology, and there is reason to believe it will continue to intensify. Children, girls as well as boys, are learning more about both at an earlier age, which means the future may provide us with leaders who are at ease with science and technology. The challenge for educators is to see that they will have the right mix of human values as well as scientific facts.

TV Makes Democracy More Expensive

"The mounting cost of elections is rapidly becoming intolerable for a democratic society, where the right to vote, and to be a candidate, is the ultimate political protection. We are in danger of creating a situation in which our candidates must be chosen only from among the rich, the famous, or those willing to be beholden to others who will pay the bills. Heavy dependence on the relatively few who can meet these enormous costs is not only demeaning and degrading to the candidates, it also engenders cynicism about the political process itself." This opinion of Robert Kennedy, former U.S. attorney general and brother of President John F. Kennedy, was quoted in a study of campaign costs, *Voters' Time*. His observations are still valid.

The cost of running for Congress has increased enormously. The well-known pollster, George Gallup, reported that the 1978 Senate and House contests had

875 candidates for 470 seats, and almost $150 million was spent on their primary and general election campaigns. This is a record amount. Two years earlier the comparable figure was below $100 million. He points out that political action committees or special interest groups contributed $35 billion or more to congressional candidates in 1978.

While legislation limits the total amount that canadidates may spend, it permits them to allocate the money as they choose. In 1976 both leading presidential candidates opted to use almost all of their funds on the mass media, with television getting most of it.

There are exceptions to every generality. Therefore it is not surprising to find politicians of modest means who have won office in the old-fashioned way: by making speeches, meeting with local leaders, shaking hands and kissing babies. Some of these candidates do win against high spending opponents who run modern media campaigns. However, such exceptions are not applicable to national elections. Despite rigorous legal controls that were passed in the post-Watergate era Robert Kennedy's concern is still relevant because political debts are an integral part of American politics. A lot of horse-trading goes on between a candidate's declaration and election night. Nonetheless, television's staggering costs have changed the campaign focus from issues to fundraising.

Television has revitalized democracy in that it broadened the base of political participation. This is interest politics at its best. But TV subverts democracy if air time is so expensive that vast sums of money are clandestinely donated by special interests in exchange for extensive leverage on winning candidates. Although this is now forbidden by new legislation the laws will be effective only if they are applied diligently. The need for vigilence is evidenced by the Senate's Watergate hearings which revealed that the Committee to Reelect President Nixon had accumulated a secret fortune, referred to by the press as a slush fund, for campaign expenses. This money financed numerous illegal activities. It was provided secretly by and sometimes extorted from special interest groups that expected or were promised political favors in return. for example, the dairy industry wanted and was granted a 1¢ increase in milk just after President Nixon had announced a price freeze. That was his thank you to the milk industry for $2 million that it contributed to his re-election campaign. One cent seems insignificant until the arithmetic is done. Using the Department of Agriculture's estimated milk consumption for 1977, a 1¢ increase would bring in about $400,000 every year; that is a good annual return on a one-time campaign investment. The complete loop led back to TV campaigning because today's expensive elections are largely a function of what broadcasters charge candidates for airtime.

Technical progress may provide additional financial relief for candidates who want access to constituents. When the United States has an abundance of national video channels, as well as narrowcasting channels that reach local audiences, it may be a buyers' market and television rates may go down. Then, candidates might be less reliant on special interests. However, dependency will not disappear altogether because interest groups are an essential part of the American political process and U.S. democracy was designed to allow for their influence.

TV Hinders Reasoned Discussion

Democracy presumes an informed citizenry and reasoned discussion. Television provides superficial information that favors imagery and immediacy of reporting over discussion. There is no intrinsic limitation that explains the superficiality of TV news. The flaw is misjudgment. Broadcasters underestimate the medium's potential to instruct and the audience's ability to learn.

TV executives did not arrive at their decision to program for the lowest common denominator without thought and careful study. The profit motive seems to require immense audiences so that TV advertisers will pay high fees: X number of dollars for every thousand viewers. Since only 15 percent of the population finish college, it was decided years ago that program content aimed at ninth-grade intelligence would yield a mass audience of potential buyers. Industry-sponsored audience research, seems to support the validity of this approach, as does the following anecdote from a California campaign.

Some years ago Pete McCloskey in California decided to give up his law practice and run for Congress. After winning a seat in the House of Representatives, he wanted to know which factors contributed most significantly to his success. He therefore commissioned a study that clearly indicated television was more influential then anything else. As McCloskey tells it, the data from his survey revealed that 5 percent of those who voted for him did so because they agreed on the issues: 10 to 15 percent voted for him because they liked his wife or they were friends; 80 to 85 percent voted for him because he looked and sounded like a good guy on TV. Even though these viewers did not know the issues, or if they did they did not agree with him, they voted for McCloskey because of his image.

This is not an isolated example of TV's image power in campaigns. Television spots run from 30 seconds to three minutes and are used frequently as political advertising by candidates because they have a proven track record of success. They are based on the psychology of subliminal persuasion, which relies heavily on repetition of simple images and concise concepts. Their brevity rules out analysis or discussion, yet they are powerful tools of persuasion, modeled after TV commercials that usually increase product sales dramatically. An interesting but negative commentary on TV news coverage of political campaigns is that several studies suggest TV spots give more information about political campaigns than does televised news. Some people worry that TV may one day put a photogenic nonentity in the White House. Others say this is an unfounded fear since we have already had nonentities in the White House and the Republic has survived their tenure.

Television is still an adolescent. As it matures it may shift from emphasis on fleeting photographic impressions to images supported by substantive reporting. Possibly the pressure of competition from other video media will promote this process, giving us more and better information during campaigns.

Another way in which television subverts reasoned discussion has been mentioned already. Journalists, especially those from the electronic press, want to have their questions answered immediately. This emphasis on prompt publicity of government action and decision making conditions viewers to believe that delay hides corruption. Although this has often been true it is also true that the democratic process requires time for debate. It would be a great service to the public and to the country if broadcasters could acknowledge and accommodate that prerequisite of our political system.

TV Influences West Coast Voting in National Elections

This deduction is based on logic rather than hard data, but the logic is compelling. Despite progress in methodology, we have not been able to isolate precisely the degree to which television influences voting behavior. Conventional wisdom suggests that the medium changes few votes because viewers watch TV to find an authority for a conclusion they have already reached, which is why they usually listen to their favorite candidates rather than to the opposition.

People like a winner. When they find one it is human nature to jump on the bandwagon, especially at the last minute when it is easier to assess the outcome. This is what happens all over the West Coast on election night as the commercial networks announce the East Coast results from polls that close three hours earlier than they do in the western time zone. Predictions are broadcast as to who will win and by what margin, almost like a track meet. In this racelike atmosphere West Coast voters are still going to the polls in significant numbers because voting is usually heavy after work. Though these voters may not have been watching TV, the predictions themselves become news that may be heard on car radios or read in the afternoon papers.

Probably a lot of resentment would be stirred up if broadcasters tried to eliminate forecasting. It might be worthwhile, however, to reconsider the idea of everyone voting during the same 24-hour period, regardless of time zones, with all polls closing simultaneously. This would produce moderate inconvenience but it would relieve broadcasters of being blamed for influencing elections almost to the point of fixing them, which is not what the networks try to do. They simply want to report results as quickly as possible and guess at the outcome if the final tally is not available.

TV Weakens Parties and Conventions

TV's nationwide coverage has given state primaries a new role in politics whose importance is greater than was foreseen or intended. Primary elections came into favor at the turn of the century as an antidote to convention nominating procedures that allowed a small group of party elites, meeting in caucus, to name candidates for public office. As a means of democratizing the secret caucus, primaries were devised so that voters could express their opinions at the polls without the exchange of political promises that characterize convention politics.

Presidential candidates are not obliged to enter state primaries. But often they will do so in key states because these have a large number of electoral votes that could swing the election, and the candidates want to demonstrate how popular they are where it counts. They also may enter primaries in states that traditionally have been weather vanes for forecasting results in national elections. Until recently, presidential candidates approached primaries with caution, much the way experienced sailors have a healthy fear of the sea, because they wanted to run only in those primaries where the chances of winning were good or where they might make a particularly strong showing.

Money was another reason why presidential candidates did not enter most of the primaries. Campaigns were and are expensive, whether they are for state or national office. Now, however, television adds a new dimension and additional expense to campaigning. Today's candidates use state primaries to get free publicity on radio and TV, but they have to spend additional money to campaign in the primaries. Of those two media TV is usually preferred because politicians want to be seen as well as heard. This was the campaign strategy that worked successfully for Jimmy Carter in his bid for the White House. When he first announced his candidacy the general reaction was Jimmy Who? By the time he had worked his way through a series of nationally televised primaries, his broad smile, flat voice, and southern accent were indisputable hallmarks of a dogged, tough-minded, well-known campaigner. Another former governor, John Connally of Texas, threw his hat in the ring as a 1980 Republican presidential candiate and, to no one's surprise, one of his strategies was to run in many primaries.

Once again the United States is confronted with TV's impact on the mounting cost of elective office. It particularly is expensive for private citizens who do not have the panoply that is available to incumbents. For example, congressional representatives have free access to government TV studios where they can prepare electronic handouts to be released to stations back home; franking privileges give them free postage for official business, which can easily be a series of selfadvertisements; it is easier for House representatives or senators to call a press conference and expect reporters to attend than it is for a political unknown; and public officials have access to inside information and contacts. Therefore, nonincumbent candidates want to gain national recognition as quickly as possible. TV, despite its phenomenal expense, is frequently their chosen means, even though each media primary may cost between $100,000 and $300,000. With that much money at stake, one might think it would be easier to buy time and avoid the hardship of campaigning. Although candidates can and do ask the TV audience for contributions, which may more than cover programming or advertising, the problem is to get on the air. There have been many instances where candidates had the money but could not buy access to TV because air time already was allocated. As politicians see it, the answer to this problem is to create newsworthy events that will get free coverage. Since camera crews often are assigned to report primary elections, modern presidential candidates want to participate in these ready-made media events. Ironically, TV covers more and more primaries because they are now important; but they have become important precisely because TV started covering them.

Another paradox is that national TV coverage seems to have lessened the risk of losing in a primary campaign. Those candidates who lose by a close margin are sometimes hailed as winners because they did better than the press expected. For instance, a Democrat who loses in a state that usually elects Republicans may be reported as a moral victor if the race was close. In such a case, one comes away from the primary with national recognition and a winner's image.

Parties are weakened by television in other ways. Candidates formerly spent much of their time finding out what party leaders want and meeting their demands. Now the candidates' principal concern is: What does TV want? How can we get free coverage on the evening news? And, especially, how can we get money to buy television time? On the one hand, TV depersonalizes campaigns because it seems to encourage a politics based on alienation, as most people meet their leaders through the media in a unidirectional process that encourages passive listening. On the other hand, television personalizes politics because viewers can see their candidates. While it is easy to confuse stagecraft with statecraft, this is more than what the public could do before TV became important in campaigns.

Television's time constraints also require politicians to conform to the medium's needs. Local speeches now are tailored for maximum effect before national TV audiences because candidates hope that an excerpt will be used on the networks' nightly news programs. This has had a salutary effect on truthfulness. Politicians find it is less easy now to tell a labor union audience that they want higher wages and then to tell big business the next day that they advocate a wage freeze. Although candidates still try to promise something for everyone, they are more circumspect about how they do it.

Anyone who has participated in or watched a party convention on TV knows how it is dominated by that medium, from deciding which city has the best support system for TV to deciding how long the nominating speeches should be. A dramatic example of television's dominant role at conventions was in Chicago 1968. Street riots and a telephone strike made TV the principal mode of communication for reporters, conventioneers, demonstrators, and the nation.

On the positive side, more extensive use of primaries can be seen as a democratizing effect. But the cost of campaigning in 30, 40, or 50 primaries is prohibitively expensive for most candidates. That is the negative side, because democracy may become a preserve of the wealthy or of those who can attract big money by promising political favors. Framing conventions and political speeches in a tighter time schedule is something that few people regret. The discipline is frequently beneficial. However, TV time is so costly that many candidates resort to brief political commercials that stress imagery and fundraising while neglecting content. This emphasis on superficiality is not consistent with democracy, which requires quality information and debate as guides to action.

TV prolongs campaigns. No other country has the extended campaigns that the United States has and, ironically, this may be due to television, which should compress rather than expand campaigns because it is a medium that transcends space and time. In early America great distances, poor transportation and inadequate communication systems justified extensive campaigns. Today, modern technology can present candidates and issues in a few weeks.

Because TV bridges campaigns, there is more continuity to the political process than there was in the past when national parties dispersed after elections. Nonetheless, American politicans declare their candidacy at least a year before voting day and start immediately to race for media coverage, preferably on television. The long lead time allows political unknowns to build up national recognition, but it builds up expenses and takes incumbent candidates away from their governmental responsibilities. This is a particularly critical problem for representatives in the House whose term is two years. They hardly arrive in Washington and start paying political favors that they promised in the last campaign when they have to start thinking about where money will come from to get reelected. One wonders how they have time to learn their job, much less do it.

Because TV news has a vast audience, it is unlikely that broadcasters will shorten political coverage. They need programming and candidates provide what one wit called inexpensive news fodder. Perhaps a more workable solution would be to extend the congressional representatives' term of office to four years and to limit the duration of campaigns.

TV Discourages Public Service

This is a conclusion that many people reached in 1972 when presidential candidate George McGovern asked his running mate, Thomas Eagleton, to withdraw from the campaign. McGovern's decision was precipitated by press reports that Eagleton had received psychological care for periodic depressions. From Eagleton's point of view, his ill health was a private matter, a past problem that had been cured. He believed he had as much right to serve the government as someone who had had pneumonia, had recuperated, and was ready for work.

Admittedly, Eagleton showed poor judgment in keeping this part of his medical history from McGovern. But he did so because he did not want it to be a career impediment, and he erroneously thought the traditional relationship of confidentiality between patient and doctor would protect him. He was wrong. By the time the imbroglio was over, and Eagleton had resigned as a vice-presidential candidate, his reputation was seriously damaged. Reporters wrote and talked about him as if he were base and beyond reform. A child molester hardly could have received worse publicity.

The Eagleton case discredits the press in general, and television in particular, because TV has the most power among the media and therefore should behave more responsibly. Most journalists reported the matter with great indignation, as if candidates must have flawless health and character. This is an unrealistic expectation. People are imperfect. If indiscretions, transgressions, and poor health are truly a part of someone's past, then it is a disservice to democracy for the press to open old wounds, impair reputations, and hound people out of office or out of running for office. Even the most heinous crime has a statute of limitations. Furthermore, freedom of the press is not our only democratic tradition. The right to privacy is also a great tradition. It includes the right to a confidential relationship between religious leaders and laypeople, doctors and patients, lawyers and clients. By what authority does the press override these personal rights?

If McGovern and Eagleton had won, would it have been so terrible to have a vice-president with an inclination to depression? It is not unheard of for leaders to be frequently, even severely, depressed. Abraham Lincoln was. His melancholia is well documented, yet it is hard to believe that democracy would have been better served if he had not been allowed to run for office because of it. A similar problem faced Winston Churchill. Yet, many people agree he was a great man, a remarkable leader, and that because of his many personal strengths England was able to hold out alone against Nazi Germany. Would England have been better off if Churchill had been barred from public service because he was depression prone?

The essential question is this: Should the public have access to every facet of people's lives if they are in government service? Usually ths answer is yes and the justification is that someone who works for the government has no right to privacy. Supposedly, this is the price of fame, glory, and public service. But what of the press that has assigned itself the task of being democracy's police officers, moral guardians, and judges? These important responsibilities are public service. Should journalists be exempt from their own guidelines? Should they be investigated, cross-examined, and have their failings and frailties publicized nationally? Why should their medical records, financial affairs, legal, personal, and professional activities be protected by secrecy? As self-appointed mediators between government and people, why should they be above scrutiny, especially since they have more power than many government officials? The answer is that they should not. But they are exempt because they control the media, which is not given to public self-examination of its limitations or questionable practices. Aside from professional journals, and newspapers that are not read by most of the general public, there is little discussion or criticism about journalists or media executives, within the media itself.

Even if the press were subject to the same possibility of intimidation through publicity that other public figures endure, the question would remain: Does it serve democracy to threaten candidates for public office with national exposure of their personal lives? As technology provides more nationwide networks, this question may become increasingly important.

It is unlikely that journalists will think turnabout is fair play. They are not likely to welcome investigation by government departments or public press councils. That leaves self-regulation, a frail reed unless it is rooted in a tradition of reasonable restraint and purpose. Press councils are more prevalent today than they used to be and citizens' groups are pressuring television executives to develop their social conscience. Perhaps a revitalized sense of responsible journalism will be a by-product of these forces. If journalists believe that the private lives of public servants are fair game for media exposure, then the same principle should apply to them because they, too, work for and profit from the public. Perhaps more good people would work in government if they did not have to fear media persecution for personal matters that do not interfere with their work.

3

DEMOCRACY AND TELEVISION

OLD MYTHS AND THEIR REALITIES

American political mythology teaches that a democratic government was established nearly two centuries ago by a group of men who met in Philadelphia. Traditional folklore neglects the fact that democracy only recently has begun to mature, that it is evolutionary, an ongoing process whose success depends upon communication systems that ensure a free flow of information. Without that infrastructure there is no informed public and no democracy. The United States has demonstrated this interdependence of technology and politics again and again, each time more convincingly. Whenever the United States tried to transplant democracy to nations whose leaders were willing, whose communication systems were weak, and whose people were uninformed about public affairs, it failed. No matter how much money, effort, or force accompanied American zeal, it was like planting fertile seed in barren soil, because the relationship of democracy to a free press is vital, not incidental. But myths die hard. A look at Philadelphia in 1787 might be instructive.

Our Founding Fathers' greatest accomplishment was to forge a more perfect union among 13 feuding states, each of which considered itself sovereign. Devising the principle of federalism, they artfully transformed dissonance into harmony by guaranteeing states' rights within the context of national community. Certain rights and policy matters fell within the pale of central government, such as the freedoms of speech, religion, assembly, and the press, the right to print money, devise foreign policy, levy taxes, regulate commerce, and so on. All other powers that were not denied specifically or that were not delegated to the national government belonged to the states. After much heated discussion, a Constitution was written to formulate this eighteenth-century version of American democracy, which was essnetially elitist.

The U.S. Declaration of Independence states that all men are created equal. But the Constitution was written in such a way that only white, male, property owners, over 21, were free, equal, and protected by law. Others might die for their country (youths under 21), build the nation's railroads (orientals), live in bondage (blacks), have their lands stolen by the government in spite of legal treaties (Indians), be treated as chattel (women and children), but they had no legal recourse for iniquities until later generations amended the Bill of Rights. Women, children, and minorities were not given the vote at Philadelphia because they did not exist politically. They had no human rights. Said differently, our forebears produced a "government of the people, for the people and by the people" that was indeed democratic for its time, but the definition of people did not include blacks, minorities, nonfreeholders, women, or children. These outcasts participated in our great political experiment much later, as technology expanded communication systems, as access to information was made available to the many as well as the few, and as new amendments were added to the first ten that originally comprised the Bill of Rights.

LOW VOTER TURNOUT AND INTEREST POLITICS

For sometime now, social critics have worried about the declining turnout for national elections. It has dropped consistently and significantly during the past 20 years, and is frequently interpreted as a sympton of democracy's decline. Only 51 percent of our eligible voters went to the polls in the 1976 presidential election, which compares unfavorably with the 80 and 90 percent turnouts in other democracies. But many countries compel citizens to participate. Punitive measures take the form of fines, loss of voting privileges, or exclusion from holding public office. Compulsion has found no favor in the United States. On the other hand, foreign elections are often scheduled for Sunday, as a matter of voter convenience, and it has been suggested that the United States might do the same. Perhaps it would be worth a try.

Some theoreticians would not like to see such a change. They argue that democracy in America works precisely because few people participate at the polls; that those who do not vote on Tuesdays should not be rewarded by a more convenient day; that the present system allows the indifferent to be excluded easily, which to them seems a beneficial effect. One reaction to this theory is that it is cynical. A more sympathetic hearing has been given to the impact of high mobility on voting habits, because many are temporarily out of town on voting day. Others have moved recently to new states and cannot vote until they meet the residency requirements for electoral participation. Each state has its own rules. In such cases voters may use an absentee ballot that can be mailed to the state from which they moved. Required registration is another impediment to voting. Some people forget about it and find on voting day that they are disqualified. Certain states have eliminated preregistration and others probably will follow suit. Some states are experimenting with registration by mail or on site at the polling booths. One thing is certain: every layer of paperwork between citizens, and the polling booth means there is less likelihood that a ballot will be cast.

One could argue that the prerequisites for voting have been around a long time and that in the good old days citizens did their duty. The implication is that today's Americans are less responsible than their forebears and that this proves democracy is weak and inappropriate to modern life. The interpretation of the good old days neglects the fact that there was considerably less mobility. So it may be that one of the key reasons for today's low voter turnout is simply that people who normally would vote are on the move. Perhaps the disheartening statistics have no deeper meaning than that.

Margaret Mead wrote about civic apathy in 1976: "The rising tide of turned-off voters is ominous. Very ominous. Hitler came to power in Germany, and Czechoslovakia was taken over by the Russians—both by legal means. If most of the people are bored, anything can happen." This was published during the presidential campaign, shortly after a debate between candidates Ford and Carter. The average audience for each of those three televised debates approximated 80 million people. This may indicate many things, but it is not a sign of political apathy. No one was compelled to watch TV. The United States is not a dictatorship where the government orders people to fill stadiums, line boulevards, or view political programs. Viewers who watched the debates (millions more heard them on radio and read about them in the print media) did so because they were turned on by politics, not off. Voting, though important, is only one indicator of interest. It is not a reliable instrument for assessing the vitality of an entire political system.

Anyone who thinks Americans are politically bored and passive should review the origin, evolution, and effects of Californians' tax revolt in 1978. Proposition 13, the Jarvis-Gann initiative, required extensive citizen participation before it qualified for the ballot.* When it was obvious that it would

---

*California citizens can initiate a law, which is what Howard Jarvis and Paul Gann did. They proposed that property taxes be lowered, and obtained the legally specified number of voter signatures to qualify that proposition for the ballot. At the next election the voters passed it into law. This procedure involves a tremendous amount of participatory politics and it could not be accomplished in a politically apathetic environment.

become a voting issue, the anti-Proposition 13 people marshaled their forces, which meant more political participation, to argue that California needs high property taxes if it is to maintain its excellent quality of life, such as fine public schools and social services. Before the campaign was over, millions of citizens had participated in the political process, explaining, writing, arranging debates and attending them, folding letters, handing out door-to-door information, watching programs, and reading articles, pro and con. It was a classic case of grass-roots politics, where the little people took on big government. Some people think the poor and minorities suffer because many social services have been trimmed, discontinued, or now require higher fees. Others note that some landlords are passing partial tax benefits on to tenants and that government departments have found ways to be cost-effective without sacrificing quality. Whether one was for or against Proposition 13, the incontestable fact is that a complex economic issue roused one of the nation's largest and most populous states to fever-pitch political activity. This campaign had close national coverage by all media. Consequently, many other states became involved in a tax revolt based on the California model.

Democracy is in better form today than when it was established. The United States has weathered two centuries of folly and adversity. Still, the freedom that Americans enjoy is envied everywhere. The Founding Fathers deserve high marks for designing a government that endures despite the foibles of human nature. Somehow voters manage to choose enough representatives who work for the common good so that liberty is maintained, the transfer of power is peaceful, and America's leadership role continues despite greivous errors in judgment.

The U.S. government's political stability is more unusual and significant than most people realize. American democracy has endured longer than most contemporary governments, despite civil, regional, and world wars, great economic depressions, many smaller convulsions, and some occasional political catastrophes. The record shows that Russia was still ruled by czars at the turn of the century; that democracy did not take hold in England until the Reform Bill of 1832 when prime ministers were empowered to rule while the crown reigned. The stage was set for the French Revolution in 1789, but violence kept the country in turmoil so that the First Republic was not established until 1792. It was only in this century that many other European nations made the transition from monarchy to representative government, including Germany, Italy, Greece, and Spain. In the orient, Japan still had an emperor until after World War II, when the transition to democracy was imposed by its U.S. conquerors. Elsewhere, China was bloody with struggles as late as the 1920s when a republic was formed. South America similarly was engaged: new governments came and went as coup after coup uprooted traditional rulers. In many parts of the world governments are democratic in name only. The press is not free and there is, essentially, only one slate of candidates for office. These governments are actually dictatorships, some more benevolent than others. But during our turbulent history, Americans have supported the idea that ultimate power belongs to the people, who have rights to freedom of speech, religion, assembly, petition, and the press guaranteed by their Constitution.

POLITICIZING LINEAR ILLITERATES

Linear illiterates are people who have trouble reading and writing. Now they can be politicized by radio and TV, the electronic press, but during the Gutenberg era, when print dominated communications, they were alienated from the political process. As technology made it possible for them to learn through broadcasting, their level of socioeconomic and political expectations rose significantly, creating what social scientists call a revolution of rising expectations. If the frustrations that typically accompany this revolution are not relieved, they can and often do lead to violence. This is what happened in the 1960s when blacks rioted throughout America's cities. A postmortem on the Watts riots suggests that blacks might not have turned to destruction if they had had access to public opinion and the authorities via TV, or if officials had done something to relieve the pressing racial problems. But institutionalized politics and the press ignored Watts until violence was used to command attention. Then the press arrived, cameras whirred, and democracy on the skids was broadcast coast to coast. How much more responsible it would have been if journalists had reported civic disorder in the making rather than waiting for it to erupt.

History supports the thesis that tolerance eventually increases as new techniques for interaction with strangers are introduced. Printing, modern transportation, and electronic communication have all helped to reduce fear and tension. Yet the same technology fuels violent struggle, such as war. We would have to be deaf, dumb, and blind not to admit that science increases the scope and intensity of destruction. However, one incontestable fact does not deny the existence of another any more than birth denies death or youth denies age. Television has been more than a source of information and entertainment for the apolitical and for linear illiterates. During the 1960s, many of them saw others like themselves use TV to capture public support for their cause and naturally they wondered: If they can do it, why not I? The medium became their weapon in a civil war for social justice.

Every program on television politicizes linear illiterates. They look at TV and wonder why others have what they do not, why they have so many clothes to put in a washing machine when all they own is on their backs. Indeed, why do others have washing machines when they do not even have running water? Why do people on TV look well groomed and healthy whereas they are unkempt, often sick, and sometimes worried about how they will get their next meal? Why is televised America white with a few blacks occasionally sprinkled in like flecks on the TV screen? In their world people are brown, yellow, black—white is the exception. This kind of wondering is normal in a country where government statistics for 1976 show 25 million Americans, 12 percent of the population, living below the official poverty line. This excludes several million institutionalized inmates and millions of military personnel. Nongovernmental estimates put poverty in the 35 to 45 million bracket. Whatever figures one uses, the problem is crucial. It is no help to say that America's poor are fewer than the poor in other countries or that ours are better off. The relevant comparison is the standard of living within the United States. Television is a daily reminder to many that good health, education, and material comfort are outside of their experience.

In the past television's entertainment programs aggravated resentment among the underprivileged by portraying the poor and linear illiterate as crooks, dope addicts, genetically stupid, ludicrous, or lazy. During the 1950s and 1960s it was rare to find women and minorities in sympathetic roles. Invariably, TV's good guys were white. Its women were usually compliant, insipid, hopelessly romantic, not too bright, unprofessional (except for nurses and teachers), and never the boss. But the worst frustrations were created when the medium ignored them completely, as if the disadvantaged and their problems did not exist. Public affairs programming reinforced the resentment. Producers assumed that minorities and women could not understand power or serious social issues. The evidence cited was that few of them held authority positions or leadership roles. Therefore they were not interviewed on television. For every Martin Luther King there were millions of silent blacks. For the American Indian, TV could find no spokesperson until the early 1970s when the American Indian Movement staged its dramatic protest at Wounded Knee. Until the oppressed became politicized and organized, they lived their lives of quiet desperation in isolated pockets of the country. Television helped them to realize their potential political strength, because TV can build a nationwide electronic community.

Things have changed in less than a generation. Racial integration is now a fact of life, even where it is accepted only grudgingly. Affirmative action programs exist even though they often work poorly or not at all. Slowly, women and minorities are climbing ladders of success in a wide spectrum of occupations, and some find room at the top, if only as tokens to placate protest. But that is all right. Symbols are important. Jackie Robinson was a terrific baseball player though many people thought he was just a showcase black. They were wrong. He was a man on point who led the way for other blacks. Now it is hard to think of American sports without thinking black as well as white. The few who make it provide hope to the many who watch, if only because their success is a resounding denial of genetic incompetence.

It was TV news coverage of street politics* that turned things around. Viewers saw that the underprivileged could be intelligent, articulate leaders.

---

*In this book, "street politics" and "media politics" are used interchangeably.

Entertainment programs followed suit. Television would have lost credibility if it continued to cast the disadvantaged in stereotype roles, as disinterested in and unable to handle power. To reflect the new reality, entertainment programs, with their immense audiences, have become carriers of democratic values. TV's most famous male chauvinist pig, Archie Bunker, had the ideal, compliant wife until Edith started to act uppity, not regularly, just every now and then. The audience loved it. Edith was legitimizing a feminist idea that women are people too. Similarly, one of the daughters in "Eight Is Enough" did not limit her horizons to becoming a nurse. The script called for her to be a doctor, whereas her older brother was not interested in going beyond high school. And, though it is still unusual for black television detectives to have white police officers working for them, the shock effect has worn off because that does occur offscreen as well as on camera.

Commercials also politicize linear illiterates. They emphasize the politics of privation. Viewers who do not have and cannot get what is advertised start to wonder: Why? Who does? Commercials create a snowflake effect. Each is separate, fragile, seemingly insignificant. But when snowflakes get together they can stop traffic, cover mountains, wreak havoc, and bring the rhythmns of society to a screeching halt. Similarly, TV ads have millions of symbols, each of which is fairly harmless, but not when one sees them every few minutes. Commercials usually are presented by healthy, educated, properly clothed, well-housed whites. To the disadvantaged viewer these symbols say the same thing: you are not part of the real world. Ads provoke desires that seem attainable, but for the poor they are like hunger on an empty stomach: gnawing away, creating desires. All societies have extremes of wealth and ours has less than many. But prior to television, the poor were not browbeaten by luxury. Now, however, it is paraded with hypnotic regularity. Most televised products are affordable to many: toothpaste, soft drinks, deodorant, cosmetics, beer, soap, cereal, and bread. They are commonly used. But the backdrop for TV ads is often expensive furnishings in lavish homes or chic restaurants. The sales pitch is made by healthy, handsome, beautifully dressed men and women, casually draped on evergreen lawns next to kidney-shaped pools, in white suburbia. These symbols of exclusion are subliminal political irritants. As our developing communication systems have disseminated information about the good life, they have also created a pressing need for democracy to expand equality of opportunity if it is to survive. People want what they see. Television is educating the underprivileged to know what is available and to feel frustrated about not having it.

TV messages give unidirectional information about the middle and upper classes. Few programs or commercials discuss poverty, exclusion, or exploitation. When the disenchanted turn to violence, no one is more surprised than those who live comfortably, whose astonishment is proportional to their insularity. Shouldn't the nation's most powerful medium also be a forum for the other America?

Television has social responsibilities that are not being met, but its executives do not want to hear about them. They are interested predominantly in their privileges. As they see it, journalists are obliged to report "what happens." This is usually said as if no decision-making process occurs before air time. Actually, TV is selective about what it reports, and selections usually ignore the poor except when their behavior is antisocial. "We give the public what it wants" is a time-worn phrase that broadcasters use to explain the lack of relevant reporting. But the underprivileged also own the airwaves from which television, cable, and satellite industrialists amass fortunes. Why should programming ignore their needs, instead of educating those who live well that inequality of opportunity exists and that it can and should be corrected?

Television advocates and teaches a politics of violence. Blacks, American Indians, anti-war demonstrators and enemies of Iran's shah had no difficulty attracting TV. Property destruction is a proven method for getting on the air. So is terror, such as hijacking and kidnapping. Once violence is set in motion, reporters appear from nowhere to cover the story. But television is silent about orderly change, such as protests against children's TV programs and the exploitative nature of televised commercials. These nonviolent protests are a social and economic struggle of enormous magnitude. Ten years ago it would have been inconceivable for the Parent-Teacher Association to bring about a meeting with vice-presidents of companies that advertise on children's programs. Yet that is what happened in 1978. Twenty of TV's leading advertisers met in Chicago with the PTA, which threatened to boycott their products if they advertised on excessively violent programs and if their commercials were either false or misleading. Similar meetings have continued in 1979 and were reported extensively in the print media, but the organization and development of this movement among media activists, educators, parents, government representatives, pediatricians, and psychologists generally has been ignored by television. The inescapable conclusion is that TV encourages violence. That is what gains access to TV and then to political power. Peaceful change, the hallmark of democracy, is treated as if it does not exist.

Street politics was not new in the 1960s and 1970s, but the televising of street politics was. There have been massive demonstrations, riots, and strikes throughout U.S. history, but TV gave a nationwide face and voice to civic disorder. Without reflecting on their part in the process, broadcasters gave extensive coverage to violent abuses of and challenges to established authority. National networks taught the techniques of organization provocation, passive resistance, and media exploitation.

As they gained experience in reporting media politics, TV executives established guidelines to avoid manipulation. Because the arrival of TV crews often intensified rioting, networks devised ways for journalists to be less conspicuous: when possible, they avoided powerful lighting, they often used unmarked vehicles, they refused to cover "spontaneous" demonstrations that were deliberately scheduled for the evening news, they resisted the temptation to have action shots repeated "just once more, for the cameras." Still, the formerly powerless successfully demonstrated that solidarity, defiance, and especially violence would win TV coverage and a serious hearing.

For example, using strategies similar to other televised protests, a group of handicapped men and women lobbied for equal rights at a 1977 San Francisco meeting of Health, Education and Welfare officials. Wheelchairs, crutches, and obvious impairments were a dramatic backdrop to the main force of their moral courage. Although the United States has no formal legislation against the handicapped, they suffer nonetheless from numerous inequities because they have been ignored. As one wheelchaired woman explained to reporters, in an obvious allusion to the blacks' demonstrations: "I don't want to move from the back of the bus to the front. I just want to be able to get on." Using a televised sit-in these demonstrators established solidarity with others like themselves throughout the nation, won public sympathy, and achieved a measure of concrete success. Since then, some new buses have been equipped to accommodate wheelchairs, civic improvements include ramps to facilitate movement where stairs ordinarily would have been the only choice, parking lots have increased reserved space for the handicapped near building entrances, and a national, government campaign has been launched along similar lines. Once again, viewers were taught by TV that personal action is meaningful. In a vast country of enormous complexity, well organized, ordinary people can effect change, especially when they have access to television.

Despite its superficiality as a news source, television has made outstanding contributions to democracy as a champion of minority rights. It is not easy to silence activists now that TV can draw national attention to injustice.

Often it is said that modern politics increases apathy, ennui, and alienation. Certainly society's problems are more complex today. But, on the other hand, political activists are better educated and equipped to handle them, particularly through the medium of interest groups that are an essential part of the American governing process. Many neglected subgroups have campaigned via TV for rights that were denied to them and some of their campaigns have been at least partially successful. The denial of civil or human rights is clearly an indictment of democracy, but even partial correction signifies that representative government is alive and well.

AN INFORMED CITIZENRY?

The immediacy of contemporary broadcasting brings more news to more people than ever before. Yet it has not brought understanding and relevance, the meaningful information upon which to act. One critic suggested that until it does so, TV news should carry a warning at the beginning and end of each program that it may be hazardous to viewers' political health. The problem is not only that televised news is superficial. It is made worse because many viewers rely on it as a primary or sole source of information about public affairs and they feel as if they understand what is happening when they see it on the screen. Television allows them to vicariously experience a disaster, participate in a demonstration, know the nation's leaders. One has the impression of learning firsthand, more deeply than through reading, because people give high credibility to eyewitness reports.

Television seldom covers the long, often dull meetings where democratic decisions are worked out. As a result, many viewers come to believe that great problems can be quickly resolved. TV has helped to produce a "turned on" generation that wants immediate experience and gratification at the flick of a switch: sex, laughter, murder, mayhem, winning, losing, and quick solutions to problems, whether they are personal or political. It is all there, instantly accessible on TV. Democracy is not like that. It is circuitous, time-consuming, and full of false starts. Broadcasters do the country a disservice with their superficial version of the news. They are wrong in thinking that people would be bored by context, history, or intelligent interpretation. Their primary concern, and as business people it is a valid one, is the bottom line. But profit making and social responsibility are not mutually exclusive. It is illusory to believe that they are. Viewers who know quality programming respond to it, and those who do not know it can be taught to appreciate it. This is the working principle on which the United States has based the people's right to know: citizens can and do learn. It is better for democracy if viewers are encouraged to do so because the ripple effect of voter ignorance is powerful in the electronic age. As the medium with the highest credibility and the largest audience, TV should provide adequate information for political action because misinformation can have staggering consequences. Televised inaccuracies can do enormous, instant damage to a person's reputation on a national or international scale: they can cause immediate, extensive, and unnecessary panic. It is the reach and instantaneity of TV that makes it imperative for televised news to be the top of the line when it comes to quality of information.

The United States was better able to withstand the effects of ignorance when the country was decentralized politically as it was in the eighteenth and nineteenth centuries. Blunders could be checked, softened, or corrected before they became widely known and caused widespread or irreparable damage. But modern America increasingly is centralized, both intellectually and politically. The possibility of one force dominating others is not as farfetched today as it was two centuries ago when people could not be mobilized instantly to action. That was the linear era when ideas were shared by word of mouth or were printed first in one medium and then another. Many weeks or months went by before events were widely known. Their effects could be prepared for or dealt with even while the news was being circulated. Major decisions were framed by extended time spans that were compatible with discussion. We do not have that luxury today.

A COURT OF LAST RESORT

American Indians talk about the history of their negotiations with the federal government as a "trail of broken treaties." Time and again U.S. officials negotiated land purchases that were inhumane and illegal, based on deception. But what could Indians do? The white man was more powerful economically and militarily. To whom could they turn for redress? In the 1970s they turned to public opinion, via televised coverage of their sit-in at Wounded Knee. And at least for several weeks they had the daily attention of authorities, journalists, and the public. TV does not produce miracles but it raised people's awareness about the conditions of poverty and neglect in which many American Indians live.

Similarly, the exploitation of migrant workers is known by many but it frequently is disbelieved because some Americans do not want to admit that in the United States people can be paid a pittance for hard labor or that the law would allow them to be fed and housed like cattle. Better to ignore the migrants, and better for the migrants to remain silent. Who would take them seriously? The American public did, when Cesar Chavez led strike after strike and television covered them. Eventually grievances were drawn up, farm labor unions were established, and some improvements can be seen. This might have been possible in the past, but it would have been harder, and improvements might not have happened so quickly.

Racism is another example of television's democratizing effects. Generations of Americans punished their slaves in cruel and unusual ways if they were even slightly rebellious. People who called themselves Christians righteously believed that black activists should be maimed, tortured, beaten, or killed outright. Eventually the force of history abolished slavery, but inhumane treatment continued wherever there was intense racism. It has always been hard for blacks to find an audience large and influential enough to help them make progress quickly. But in the television age they know how to find that audience—by planning public, massive demonstrations that are symbolic, colorful, dramatic, and, if necessary, violent. That attracts cameras and rivets the attention of authorities. It is a proven method.

Television has become increasingly the people's court of last resort. This particular role was not chosen deliberately by electronic journalists; it is a spillover from their work in reporting events. But television's acceptance of this responsibility has helped to broaden equality of opportunity and make democracy more meaningful.

CREATING THE NEWS

When television was a young medium, many of its journalists came from print and radio. They brought along the unfortunate practice of occasionally creating events instead of simply reporting them. Newspaper photographers were accustomed to shooting several pictures, often asking that action be restaged "just once more for the camera." Usually there was no intent to deceive. The goal simply was to make a story better by having appropriate pictures. The same reasoning was transferred to television, and it was not until the many riots of the 1960s that people began to question the practice of restaging a confrontation because the camera crew had arrived late or missed the action, thereby creating a rerun of an event rather than reporting the event itself.

Creating news is not a deception limited to journalists. Demonstrators have also learned to schedule "media events" at broadcasters' convenience, preferably in time for the evening news, preparing them in a suitable TV format: simple messages, dramatic action (if it erupts into violence that might be even better), clear symbols, articulate spokespersons, and some obvious physical difference between Us and Them. A classic example of media exploitation occurred when the American Indian Movement seized Wounded Knee to protest the Indians' second-class citizenship.

4

TELEVISION AND TYRANNY

FROM PENNY SHEETS TO POWERFUL INSTITUTIONS

Until the eighteenth century every government had its own methods and reasons for trying to restrict information to a privileged few, primarily because the masses are controlled more easily if they are ignorant. After winning independence from England, America broke with that tradition and struck out on a new path that guaranteed its citizens a free press. The First Amendment to the U.S. Constitution says:

> Congress shall make no law respecting an establishment of religion, or prohibiting the free exercise thereof; or abridging the freedom of speech, or of the press; or the right of the people peaceably to assemble, and to petition the Government for a redress of grievances.

These few and simple words ensure press freedom and summarize the essense of American democracy, which is respect for human rights. However, journalism's once penny sheets are now powerful institutions. Using the First Amendment as a shield against inquiry and accountability, today's journalists threaten the delicate balance between liberty and license, between personal independence and televised tyranny.

A careful analysis of the American Constitution reveals certain assumptions about human nature and government. Its authors were aware of and distrusted human frailty. They understood and agreed with the time-worn axiom that power begets itself and tends toward tyranny. Having freed themselves recently from the yoke of an English tyrant, America's Founding Fathers decided against relying on human nature to preserve liberty. Rather, they devised a series of mechanisms to separate, check, and balance authority so that no one power center could dominate the others. Therefore, Congress makes laws that are implemented by the executive and interpreted by the judiciary; the legislature appropriates funds but they are allocated by the president; the executive branch of government appoints chief justices but only with the advice and consent of the Senate; all representatives act on behalf of their constituents but the people are sovereign and may vote their representatives out of office. This ingenious balancing and checking of powers works like a fulcrum on which all aspects of American democracy turn.

Only by distorting the First Amendment can one interpret it as giving absolute freedom to the press. On this point, the Constitution addresses itself only to the legislature: "Congress shall make no law . . . abridging the freedom of the press." The executive, the judiciary, and the nation's sovereign, the people, are not similarly admonished. These words do not empower journalists to be above the law, to invade privacy, or to usurp governmental functions. Although the press has been, in many cases, a guardian of the public interest, this is a self-assigned role that has no constitutional legitimacy. Rather, it has evolved over time and is rooted in custom. Perhaps it would be instructive to consider religion in the same context as the press since the First Amendment also guarantees its freedom, with words that are strikingly similar: "Congress shall make no laws respecting an establishment of religion or prohibiting the free exercise thereof." Religion has not appointed itself as a guardian of the public interest. If it did it would be hard put to justify such a move on constitutional grounds.

To argue that freedom of the press means an absence of restraint is to fly in the face of the constitution's fundamental premise that unchecked power is tyrannous. Had the authors of the constitution foreseen that the media would become virtually a fourth branch of government, they might have applied the same logic that pervades the rest of the Constitution and restrained the press through some accountability mechanism such as is applied to each of the three governmental branches. But they did not anticipate the press as a vast power center. Eighteenth-century printers were among the oppressed, not the privileged, and since America's new leaders were looking for meaningful symbols to enshrine their hard-won freedom, what better choice could be made than a press whose independence is guaranteed constitutionally against the vagaries of lawmakers? Two hundred years ago, freedom of the press was a singular symbol of madness or courage, an historic first.

Though it is commonplace today, it was inconceivable in 1789 that the United States would have a national video "newspaper" dominated by three commerical networks whose combined audience (one-fourth of the population) can be reached instantly and simultaneously. This is what the evening TV news does, Monday through Friday. Television derives its awesome political power from the interaction of several forces: a vast, simultaneous audience, instant access, high credibility, nationwide scope, its ephemeral nature (now you see it, now you don't—which makes it difficult to check), and negligible accountability. The last two in particular explain why TV is one of the most credible authorities in the United States.

These factors function in the context of broadcasting's extensive financial empire, whose scope and impact rival other big businesses in a unique way. Despite immense wealth and power, other multinationals cannot investigate broadcasting's affairs and make their findings public on a global scale under the guise of legitimate investigative reporting. Aside from investigative bodies such as the CIA, FBI, and the police, the press is the only big business that can do this as part of their job. They have social acceptance for it because the media have conditioned people to think of the press as a version of Britain's loyal opposition, the public's watchdog.

The press knows how important it is for people in a democracy to be informed of government activities all along the decision-making route while there is still time for opinion to affect policy. "The public's right to know" is a valid principle, a logical extension of the people's sovereignty. But frequently it is misinterpreted by journalists who sometimes use it as a passport to probe and push, question and challenge, admonish and advise, pressure and punish everyone and anyone doing business as government. No quarry is too small or great for the media to test their mettle and no medium has the power that television is believed to have.

TELEVISION, TYRANNY, AND DEMOCRACY

Tyranny is the arbitrary use of power in the absence of accountability. This describes television.

Before 1968 when Vanderbilt University in Nashville, Tennessee started its Television News Archive, there was no reasonable way to verify the entirety of most televised newscasts. Though their effects might be felt throughout the country and beyond, the ephemeral nature of TV news made it nearly impossible to review the record. Therefore, unlike newspaper reporters, electronic journalists were not held accountable for what they said, implied, or the way they used visuals.

Although each commercial network maintains archives, they are incomplete, difficult to use, and seldom open to the public. Until recently, one could not retrieve news programs as complete entities. Even as late as the 1960s, most news was erased within two weeks of being broadcast so that expensive and space-consuming videotapes could be reused. Film clips might be cut up and filed according to subject as stock material for future broadcasts. Verbatim transcripts of an entire news program were a rarity in the early years of television and audio tapes seem to have been kept sporadically. Certain materials were preserved if they were judged to be historically important. For a researcher to review a particular, complete newscast from, say, 1962, the following procedure would have to be used: (1) Ask the station if there is a transcript. There might be but it is likely that the commercials and anchor's part of the program will not be transcribed. (2) See if there is a complete audio tape of the program: doubtful but possible. (3) Using the news program's script as a guide (or the audio tape's written index to the program's contents), retrieve each film segment from the various places in which they are filed. (4) Splice these together. (5) Rerun the final product, which most likely will not contain commercials, the anchor's commentary, or all of the news that was broadcast because portions will have been discarded as unimportant for reference. This research procedure is complicated, time-consuming, and costly. Few people did it. Therefore the commercial networks seldom were held accountable for what they broadcast and so had enormous, nationwide, unchecked political power.

Broadcasters shape our view of reality not only by reporting events but most particularly by selecting those stories that will be reported and those that will be ignored. Several factors influence their choice: newsworthiness of the event, technical matters, the human factor, money, and politics.

"If it wasn't reported it didn't happen." That bit of journalistic folklore is a pithy summary of TV reality. The power to decide what the public will know (setting the political agenda) is often exercised without reference to viewers' or society's needs. Whether or not an event is reported may have more to do with technical reasons than with newsworthiness, a vaguely defined term that usually means the subjective opinions of reporters and editors. Important events may be excluded from television's evening news because the satellite did not work, the film was processed incorrectly, the plane with the film footage did not arrive on time, or there was some other nonnewsworthiness problem.

Then there is the human factor. Are the producers interested in the reporter's story? Is the report offensive to big advertisers, affiliate stations, powerful politicians, certain executives within the network? These considerations often lead to self-censorship. They are invisible, subtle and sometimes unconscious but they shape the news. Why prepare material for a story when the network's prevailing values will not accommodate it? How much easier and practical to select another event and raise it to the status of news.

Money is an obvious determinant of what gets broadcast. The commercial networks are profit-making multinationals, big business in the biggest sense of the word. The bottom line has a lot to do with whether money is allocated to cover one event or another.

Politics is another key factor. Politics simply means power relationships. These are not limited to government. There are network politics, personal politics (among competing colleagues), the politics of economics. They leave their imprint of censorship just as clearly as an imprimatur. For instance, how curious that commercial networks do not show documentaries about television, or broadcast news about their own vast empires with the same avid interest that they have in oil companies. Both industries, broadcasting and oil, are multinationals; both are powerful, with broadcasters having more power because they control an important information source for most Americans; and yet television ordinarily neglects itself as a newsworthy subject. When CBS sued Vanderbilt University in the early 1970s the issues included freedom of speech, freedom of the press, and TV's absence of political accountability. The networks gave them no air time to these issues on their version of reality. Similarly, in 1978 and 1979 a nationwide grass-roots movement grew to protest excessive violence and sex in TV programming, as well as certain aspects of proposed revisions for the Communications Act. The full panoply of TV drama was there: violence, sex, demonstrations, mom, dad, and the kids, celebrities from TV, film, and politics. What could be more relevant in a nation where television is on for seven hours a day in the average home? Yet money, prestige, and raw political power censored this protest movement from the screen. Why should the public worry its empty little head about matters that are best handled by TV executives? Give the viewers more footage about riots and plane crashes. That should keep them nicely diverted from network censorship or other matters relevant to their daily lives about which they might care deeply if they had access to the information.

~ The comparison of television to tyranny is appropriate. Tyrants control the source and flow of information just as the networks control TV, which is the sole source of information about public affairs for many Americans. Knowledge is still power whether it comes to us instantly, simultaneously, and electronically, as it does today, or whether it is transmitted orally, as in biblical times. A democratic society needs adequate economic, social, and political news.

It needs debate, not submission. Although the hardware exists for bidirectional communication between viewers and program participants, the usual time lag that separates technological innovation from institutional change means that it will be years before the audience takes an active part in news broadcasts. Meanwhile broadcasters encourage intellectual lassitude among viewers because they think that objectivity would be impaired if editors asked themselves: what do responsible citizens need to know? Objectivity is a journalistic myth. There should be guidelines for providing in-depth knowledge of social, economic, and political events if democracy is to function well.

High credibility and unassailable power are two other traits of tyranny. People are passive before tyrants because tyrannical power is overwhelming and the prevailing belief is that opposition is impossible. Television's high credibility as a news source is explained largely by accident and human nature, not by high quality reporting. Quite by chance it became our national newspaper because people believe what they see, accepting uncritically what is shown. Why not? Until recently there was little possibility of contradicting television news, which meant it was difficult to oppose the networks' power.

Television calls itself a window on the world. It seems to be everywhere and to know something about everything, from sports to space-age technology. In addition to being omnipresent, it gives the impression of being omniscient because it is not verified easily. These are the attributes of a deity: omniscience, omnipresence, and irrefutability. Together, they create an aura of superiority that encourages acceptance of the idea that First Amendment protection allows journalists to be privileged citizens because they have appointed themselves guardians of the public interest, as if the press had no self-interest, corporate or otherwise. Broadcasters tend to see themselves as dedicated, altruistic, and beyond reproach. They are inclined to resent evaluation or criticism of their work as a constitutional violation.

TV journalists argue that television is not much different from other media in its presentation of news because editorial judgment is exercised in all reporting. Therefore, if TV is tyrannical, so is print and radio. Wrong. Television news enjoys a unique political role in terms of vast audience, instant access, simultaneous reception, and excellent credibility ratings. This cannot be repeated too often. These qualities put TV in a class by itself. Standards for applying the First Amendment must therefore be different.

A TYRANT TYRANNIZED

Television, too, is tyrannized by time, technology, and its own decision makers.

If you have ever tried to deliver an extremely complicated message in a three-minute phone conversation, you have some idea of how difficult it is to report complex events on the TV news where time is tight and the format is show-and-tell. Precious seconds are used for visuals and even if there is a voice-over accompanying commentary, the image dominates: one picture is still worth 1,000 words.

The rule of thumb for getting air time seems to be: if the pictures are good, we'll run it, even though the story may be irrelevant to most viewers; if the pictures are poor or nonexistent, but it's an important story, we'll give it a one-minute slot or ignore it altogether. When journalists are forced to think pictures, write pictures, and talk pictures, the net effect is minimal information and abundant superficiality. If the televised evening news were printed as aired, it would take less column space than the front page of a good newspaper. The insidious effect of this emphasis on images is that nonvisual stories get buried or . excluded, even if the public needs to know about them.

Equipment and budgets are also tyrants, though continuing miniaturization is easing technology's tyranny. Television hardware is still relatively heavy and therefore video journalists ordinarily work with camera crews. The logistics of getting everyone's schedules together, while holding costs to an acceptable level, means that program content is dictated by organizational considerations rather than by newsworthiness or relevance.

Are these problems different from other media? Yes, vastly. Print journalists can go more places less conspicuously. Their only equipment is a notebook. They do not rely upon a team to accompany them in order to get the basic story. But TV crews are clustered in major metropolitan areas rather than in America's heartland or near its borders, which is why televised America is a caricature of reality. It is the classic story of organizational dynamics dictating behavior.

TELEVISED TYRANNY?

It is not unthinkable that television could be used tyrannically in our relatively centralized society. The film *Network* satirized this theme, but many professional journalists were not amused. It came too close to home. They thought it was perfectly plausible for an anchorman-turned-demagogue to manipulate viewers, as the protagonist in the film did when he told them: "I'm mad as hell and I won't take it any more!" He then tells his TV audience to open their windows and shout the same message. They do. In city after city, across the nation, windows are thrown open and people yell into the night air: "I'm mad as hell and I won't take it any more!" It's done as if by reflex. One would think they were programmed psychologically, which they were by having watched TV night after night, accepting whatever political agenda and interpretations were given to them by their favorite anchorman.

Nationwide thought control via TV is not unthinkable. The technology is there. The audience passivity is there. The credibility is there. Many viewers need to believe in someone who seems to be an authority and TV journalists meet this need for millions. In the 1970s a national poll showed that CBS's anchorman, Walter Cronkite, was the most trusted person in America. Surprising? Not really. He looks like a father figure right out of central casting: suitably mature, graying appropriately, unabrasive, soft-spoken, unruffled, knowledgeable about many things, and thoroughly dependable (no matter where you are in the United States he will be there with you for the evening news). Like an amiable diety who is above it all, "Uncle Walter" brings us the cataclysmic and the microscopic, all with the same detached calm. We feel comfortable with him. We "know" him. For nearly a generation he has been a guest in our homes. Of course we trust him! Presidents come and presidents go, but Walter remains like the one fixed spot in a moving universe, symbolizing stability and integrity.

People in search of authority figures find TV is a logical choice. With a twist of the wrist one is told what is important and how to think about it. The networks disguise the fact that Americans pay for programs and broadcasters encourage us to think that what they offer is free TV whereas newspapers and magazines cost money. When we leave the warm glow of our television screens we know that we know what those in the know are talking about. The next day we talk about the same things. In brief, we are programmed.

Millions of viewers participate in political life solely on the basis of what they have learned from TV. That is a serious problem for democracy. Today's highly technical society requires an understanding of complexities, human as well as scientific. But TV is consecrated to simplicities. It reduces ideas to the lowest possible common denominator (lower than necessary) in order to attract the largest possible audience for its advertisers.

Will commercial networks assume a more mature outlook on their responsibilities to democracy? Probably not. Public interest has seldom interested broadcasters unless they were forced to think about it. But they may be forced to think about it soon, for two reasons: technology will give us many more channels, thereby increasing competition and diminishing the broadcasters' monopoly; the natives are restless: citizens' groups may pressure broadcasters into thinking about viewer needs.

MEDIA CROSS-OWNERSHIP

Television's tyrannous potential is greatly increased because of media cross-ownership. Each of the three commercial networks owns and operates five television stations and several radio stations (AM and FM) in the top 50 broadcasting markets. The number of stations owned is limited by law. Translated into money, this means that the three commercial networks' TV stations (15 in all) take most of America's TV broadcasting profits even though they are generated by several hundred television stations. The networks also own or have investments in other media such as newspapers, magazines, book publishing, cable TV, satellites, films, records, and educational materials. The cross-ownership is even more complex than it seems because it flows from the other direction as well: many publishing companies, magazines, newspapers, film studios, and record companies own or have investments in TV and radio stations.

And then there are the affiliates. Most TV stations choose to affiliate with one of the three networks, while some remain as independents, and others have joined forces to establish a countervailing power to ABC, CBS, and NBC (for example, Multi-media Network). Nearly half the radio stations are Big Three affiliates, with networks supplying programs and advertisements while local stations supply air time. This allows local stations to keep their production expenses down and it gives the networks access to a nationwide audience for advertisers. From the commercials, affiliates get an agreed-upon cut of the gross income, the size of which depends on whether a station operates in a major or minor market area (defined by audience potential). Both programs and ads are transmitted over private, closed-circuit lines (called networks) that are leased for this purpose from the telephone company. All an affiliate has to do is plug in to its network and the software (programming, news, ads) will be fed to it. By law, an affiliate can refuse any program that displeases it, and several do this with some regularity.

Most affiliates accept the network news feed because it is costly and impractical for them to gather national and foreign news. This causes a fundamental political problem. The three networks' ownership of 15 TV and 21 radio stations in the major markets (say New York, Los Angeles, Philadelphia, Boston, and Washington D.C.), plus affiliation with hundreds of stations that rely upon the networks for national and international news, plus ownership of other media, give broadcasters a degree of unchecked political power that a relatively small group of people should not have in a democracy.

In the United States we are at a stage in the evolution of communications where broadcast monopoly, cross-ownership of media, and technology have produced a sameness of news for millions of Americans. This is contrary to the competition of countervailing ideas that provides diversity of opinion and keeps democracy strong.

Martin Seiden, a media critic who often does research for the television industry, argues that TV has no extraordinary powers since there are other forms of media to which people have ready access: radio, newspapers, magazines, educational institutions, and public discussions. But he invalidates his argument, as do others sharing his view, by treating TV as if it were simply an extension of print journalism. This ignores the medium's unique qualities and the fact that a large part of the television audience has difficulty reading, which effectively means they have no access to other media besides radio.

LINEAR ILLITERACY, TV, AND POLITICAL POWER

There are 23 million Americans who are functionally illiterate. That conclusion comes from the *Adult Performance Level Final Report*, issued by the University of Texas at Austin in 1977. Their analyses were not confined to reading and writing, but also included competency in simple tasks such as interpreting employment notices, completing job applications, reading and understanding check-cashing policies, writing to excuse a child's absence from school, addressing an envelope, and reading a train or plane schedule. In other words, one out of five adults in the United States cannot apply intelligence effectively to tasks that require reading, writing, and uncomplicated analysis. But many of those same people do have the right to vote and to otherwise participate in the political process (for example, pressure groups). If they were manipulated effectively, say via TV, they could be a powerful force.

Of the functional illiterates who are now apolitical, how many will continue to be passive in the future? Who knows? What we do know is that many of them cannot be written off as too stupid to learn if they are given the opportunity. Many immigrants arrived in this country without knowing how to read, write, do arithmetic, or even speak the language. Some of them went on to become leaders in their chosen field.

Is it realistic to think that functional illiterates will see the good things of life on TV everyday but will not want them for themselves or for their children? History does not support this view. People want to have what appears to be attainable. Once they realize that their horizons are limited by others rather than by their own capacities, they can be expected to press for social change. This may take place in an evolutionary way, accompanied by occasional localized violence that is defused through compromise, or, if their rising expectations are not taken seriously, it could mean more general rebellion.

Our have-nots belong to different races, ethnic groups, sexes, and religions, but a common characteristic is that many of them refuse to have not. Human ingenuity knows no bounds when it comes to upward social, economic, and political mobility. Yesterday's impoverished and ignorant will often produce tomorrow's professionals. Americans have no basis in history or logic for believing that people excluded from power will accept supinely a spectator role. Unless some appropriate steps are taken to circumvent it, we can expect a restructuring of democracy in America, catalyzed by chaos.

Television's omnipresence adds to its power. It is no longer surprising that 98 percent of American households have TV, that half of those have two sets, or that TV is on for six to seven hours a day in the average home (though it should be remembered that a functioning TV set does not necessarily mean a functioning mind is watching it—sometimes the TV is just on as background noise). What does stagger the imagination is that children spend more time watching TV than they spend in the classroom; that TV, an entertainment medium, uses a relatively small percentage of its broadcast schedule to cover public affairs and yet it is the most powerful news medium; that its reporting is superficial and distorted, yet it enjoys the highest credibility among news sources.

Television is used extensively by functional illiterates who are generally poorer than other people. Lack of funds is one reason why years of their lives are spent watching TV. (Bill Small, a CBS news executive, says "... the average American male will spend the equivalent of 3,000 full days, roughly nine years of his life, watching television.") But we deceive ourselves if we think the poor are not being politicized by television. Social and political values permeate all broadcasts, and TV develops a mind-set in its viewers even when the context seems innocuous. One example will illustrate the point. TV stereotyped blacks for a generation: they were slapstick comedy types, song-and-dance people, humble and obedient servants, or were cast as criminals, shiftless, ignorant, and unreliable. Simultaneously, in the same programs, black viewers saw how whites lived. Advertisements as well as program content told them what was available. They learned from television that violence will attract national attention. They learned to stage their own violent drama, using property damage to command attention to their needs, neglect, and exploitation. Finally, they were listened to. Much of the TV stereotyping has changed. Blacks are now cast as intelligent, hard working, and as capable leaders. Real iniquities still remain. Blacks have higher unemployment, lower education, and fewer opportunities than do whites, but some progress is being made.

DISTORTING REALITY

Though television's significance as a social force generally is acknowledged, there is a wide variety of opinion about its effect on behavior. As in much of the literature about human motivation, authorities disagree about TV's impact. The problem is muddled further by broadcasters who insist, when it serves their purpose, that TV is a benign product of technology, a neutral conduit for information that is used objectively to report the day's news. That is pure nonsense. No one reports objectively. Everything exists in a context, in relation to other things or people. Reporters cannot deal with all facets of reality. A pencil was once a plank of wood, which was once a tree, which had been part of a forest, which was rooted in and nourished by the land, which was part of a region that produced that kind of tree, and so on. From the myriad details that comprise the context, journalists choose, according to their subjective values, certain aspects to emphasize. They abstract from reality the things they want to report as news.

To the naked eye, television does seem to have no filters between image and viewer to manipulate events. However, what we see is often not what is. A lot goes on in the editing process: additions, deletions, juxtapositions of things that did not happen sequentially, synchronization of words with pictures that occurred at different times, and inserts of film footage from the files that were taken on occasions other than the one being reported. Through the magic of technology, a finished product may look untouched. Distortion of reality is something at which television excels. This is not surprising since it is primarily an entertainment medium where the ability to create illusion is highly prized and practiced daily.

Network news departments constantly struggle to keep themselves separate from the show biz side of TV, but temptations are many, the Nielsen ratings dominate program survival and human nature is frail. If a few illusions would increase the program's audience, who's to worry? For example, reverses are generally used during interviews to improve visual dynamics by letting viewers see the reporter as well as the person interviewed. Usually this does not detract from the substance of the report but it is deception. No one tells the audience that the reporter was filmed or taped on two separate occasions: once during the actual interview and then alone, often in the TV studio. The same effect could be achieved with two cameras shooting at different angles, but that requires more money and personnel for each assignment. It is less cumbersome and costly to have reverses. Dan Schorr, former CBS correspondent, tells how Bill Paley, Chairman of CBS, had complimented him on his cool during a particularly difficult interview. Paley noticed that neither stress nor the intensely hot television lights produced a drop of perspiration on his furrowed brow. Schorr could not believe it. Was the Chairman of CBS saying that he did not recognize a reverse when he saw one; that he did not know Schorr's cool was the result of a second take and splices made in the lab? He was. When Schorr told him, Paley reacted with anger and ordered that such deceptions be stopped, which they were for a time.

The voice-over is another TV technique that can cause distortion. It is a running commentary by a correspondant against a photographic background. This allows a reporter to summarize an event while avoiding the time-consuming and costly method of interviewing the people involved and letting them speak for themselves. Because viewers see pictures or artwork in the background, the report takes on a you-are-there quality that adds to its credibility.

We are told that the camera never lies. But it does, depending on how it is used. Photography can capture atypical, unflattering behavior such as a person dozing off during a speech or chewing gum. That kind of photography is not objective, it is image-commentary, much more devastating than words. In a voice-over the producer may choose visuals that slant the news. Not long ago a common complaint was that TV used wide arrows to emphasize a downturn in the economy and narrow ones to show an upswing. The speculation was that the audience might find the news more interesting if adversity were emphasized.

Broadcasters shake their heads when these things are discussed. They rightly point out how incidental, accidental, occasional, and unimportant each one is by itself. Here again, the snowflake principle applies: when snowflakes get together they can paralyze society. With respect to television, incidents may be minor, but they can be effective and subtle. Therefore, they should be examined for frequency and patterns, not as singular happenings, to see if manipulation is occurring.

In another context the press would see this as making very good sense. Any time the government does something that journalists interpret as a threat to their freedom there is a storm of protest. And with good reason. It is not that every bit of interference has equal weight, but the price of freedom is constant vigilance. Journalists want to be sure that the occasional does not become the norm, that a minor infringement on their independence is checked before it sets a precedent for future intervention. Similarly, the public must be on guard against manipulation of the news. It is important to stress television's lack of objectivity primarily because the medium's you-are-there quality disarms critical viewing. One accepts too readily what one sees.

BELIEF AND POWER

An impressive example of how credibility heightens power is found in Anthony Sampson's book, *The Seven Sisters*. He tells how the oil producing and exporting countries (OPEC) became a formidable political and economic power when they finally organized their interests. Sampson says:

> . . . the puzzle was not so much why . . . the oil producing countries became a successful cartel, but . . . why this victory had not happened earlier. The sovereign states, with their own precious resources, had taken a long time to awaken to the need to . . . combine, to confront the companies which purchased oil. . . . As one Saudi explained, *"it was not until we realized our strength that we had our strength."* (emphasis added)

Belief precedes power and legitimizes it. Sampson goes on to quote the director of the oil producing countries' Kuwait Fund:

> . . . we got as great a shock as you did. We thought we were pygmies facing giants. Suddenly we found that the giants were ordinary human beings; and the Rock of Gibraltar [the purchasing companies] was really papier mache. . . . it was like coming of age. We were amazed to discover that what we said and did made a difference.

That is precisely what must happen in America if TV is not to endanger democracy: the public must come of age and realize that they own the airwaves. The hidden tax on every TV-advertised product is what pays ABC's Barbara Walters $1 million a year in salary, as well as the other expenses connected with TV from minicams to satellites. Therefore, the public should have more say about what they see and how it is presented. There is no reason for viewers to sit back and let broadcasters run the show. The bottom line shows high profits because the public pays the bill. There is an old political maxim: "whoever holds the purse has the power." American television's purse is held by the public but they, like OPEC, must realize they have power if they are to use it effectively.

Our history, and that of most nations, spills over with examples of people who were persuaded that the gods or genetics did not destine them to enjoy the good things of life or to help shape events that affected them directly. They were taught and they believed that it was their fate to do the bidding of others who had the trappings of power. As information becomes more accessible, it is increasingly difficult to convince the disadvantaged that they are not as good, or potentially as able, as many of their leaders. In tandem with communications development we have seen radical social, economic, and political changes in every part of the world. More accessible information helps people to realize that they have possibilities for growth, which is what the ruling classes do not encourage them to know about themselves.

American democracy rests on the belief that citizens should have access to quality information. Television rests on the belief that profits are proportional to the number and kind of viewers who are sold to advertisers for so many dollars a thousand. Therefore, the name of the game is to draw a bigger audience than other networks. And because television is largely entertainment, it is easy to touch up the news and public affairs with a bit of show biz so that program ratings and advertising revenues will rise. We have already seen this in the "happy talk" format that is used by some local TV stations. Network newscasters say it will never happen to them. Maybe not. They have a long history of being serious about their work.

Belief is a powerful thing. People will accept what they see on TV because they believe it is a reflection of reality even if it clearly contradicts their personal knowledge or experience. The explanation for this is largely cyclical: TV has become an authoritative source because viewers have given it that authority by believing it is objective: ("the camera doesn't lie," "I've seen it with my own eyes"). The attitude that is brought to the television screen is not much different from the way that unsophisticated people think and act with regard to print. Until they learn better many readers think that something is true if it has been published. With instruction, readers usually come to realize that nothing is objective. That is the nature of knowledge: it has perspective, a bias. With experience people learn that eminent authorities in the same specialty; who are equally honest, can come to contradictory conclusions about the same data. With broadcasts the situation is not much different. Some news and public affairs programs are more balanced or fair in handling facts and events than others. Sometimes TV journalists misunderstand and therefore misinterpret events. And some journalists are, pure and simple, liars. Since film and videotape lend themselves to laboratory modification and other forms of distortion, it is easy to exploit the human tendency to believe that what one sees is what there is. The problem has been acute particularly with regard to television because the absence of archives meant that the record could not be checked.

TELEVISION AND BEHAVIOR

Despite the difficulty of measuring television's effects on behavior and value formation, it would be a great disservice to society if we did not pursue the problem, or, if in the absence of accurate scientific methodology, we ignored our everyday observations and common sense. For example, broadcasters deny that television violence teaches or catalyzes behavioral violence. They say the studies that suggest such a relationship are not verifiable and are therefore invalid. Yet the same executives continually assure manufacturers that a 30-second spot (advertisement) will increase sales. Usually they are right. Broadcasters may cite instances where TV ads have failed, but these are obviously exceptions, otherwise TV could not have charged more than $300,000 for each commercial minute during the 1978 Superbowl. Advertisers pay that princely price because the overall evidence shows that TV is a powerful sales tool. It does affect buying behavior. We can deduce, therefore, that it does affect other behavior. Naturally, broadcasters do not want to admit that TV's power is more immediate and far-reaching than other power centers for someone might suggest that democracy therefore requires it to be held more closely accountable to the people.

GOVERNMENT CONTROL

Television is regulated partially by the federal government as is almost every private enterprise in America from food and drugs to space exploration. But, since TV news and public affairs programming come under the constitutional guarantee for a free press, there has been continual debate about the degree to which that regulatory power should be exercised. Understandably, broadcasters believe it should be minimal or nonexistent. They and many of their sympathizers realize that the government itself engages in press activities under the guise of public relations by disseminating films, articles, books, reports, and press releases that often are passed out as news instead of as government propaganda. This was carefully analyzed, with a definite antigovernment bias, in a CBS documentary, "The Selling of the Pentagon," which reported that millions of tax dollars are spent every year by the government to promulgate its policies and improve its image. Broadcasters argue that this is all the more reason why the electronic press should be deregulated. However, many media critics see government as the only institution with enough power to guarantee that television will be used for public service as well as for profit making. Their argument is supported by history, for the record shows that broadcasters tend to neglect their civic responsibilities in the absence of coercion. Proregulation people stress that the airwaves belong to the public and are licensed only conditionally to broadcasters.

Both arguments have merit. But in the final analysis it may help to remember that the people are the government. Institutions, such as the presidency, judiciary, and legislature are not the only way for them to express their will. People can also exercise some control over broadcasting through interest groups, public discussion, and press councils; by insisting that electronic literacy be taught in schools; by advocating television archives; and by supporting public television. These methods may be effective alternatives to expanding institutionalized control, which could be tyrannous. For example, the Nixon administration feared and distrusted the press. Television particularly nettled Nixon, and during his tenure presidential authority was illegally used to curtail its power. President Nixon's strategy for containing the press is an example of the temptations that confront federal authorities and why government regulation of broadcasting should be exercised with care in a democratic society.

Nixon knew that our centralized commercial networks, with their nationwide audiences and high credibility, could be a countervailing power to his own. Therefore, he developed a plan to divide and conquer the industry as a whole, including public TV. Of the two, public television was an easier quarry because it relies on the federal government for part of its fragile funding. Not surprisingly, Nixon's tactics reflected the power of the purse. He decided to withhold money unless the following "recommendations"' were accepted: appoint Nixon sympathizers as officers to the Corporation for Public Broadcasting (public broadcasting's parent organization; this was done, giving Republicans an eight to seven majority); discontinue controversial public affairs programs and focus instead on education; have balance within each program instead of within a series of programs and instead of relying on the right to reply; and decentralize public television. To no one's astonishment, once the Republicans controlled the Corporation for Public Broadcasting in 1973, they withheld financial support from several programs that discussed controversial topics. And, while the decentralization scheme gave local stations more autonomy, it also decreased public TV's national power.

Commercial television was not as vulnerable because its funding is primarily from advertising, which is independent of government. However, the networks have always chafed against federal regulatory licenses because they can be revoked after three years if certain ill-defined public interest services are not provided. (Actually, licenses are rarely revoked.) Nixon therefore realized that the license was his leverage. He offered a five-year license (which has not gone into effect) if the industry would allow their affiliates more freedom in choosing programs. This was the same ploy he had used with public television, ostensibly advocating local independence and effectively undermining national power. The commercial networks usually presented a package of programs to local stations who were obliged to accept all of them. Affiliates disliked the arrangement because it did limit their freedom of choice. But belonging to a national network had important financial advantages and they accepted the package system as a tradeoff for the affiliation. One may argue that the networks were tyrannical and that the system was long overdue for reform. However, liberalism was not Nixon's motive. To weaken further the networks' centralized power, Nixon insisted that program production should be the work of many sources, rather than controlled by the networks. Again, this has democratic effects, but it also weakens television in relation to the administration's power. Nixon also prepared his now-famous enemies list, which included television journalists who were to be singled out for harassment by the Internal Revenue Service, whose close analyses of income tax returns can become abusive. The Federal Bureau of Investigation also was encouraged to put journalists under surveillance, which included illegal phone taps. And the Federal Communications Commission allegedly was used when the *Washington Post* tried to renew its broadcast license for a television station that it owns. Its petition for renewal was challenged. (The *Post* is a paper for which Nixon had a particularly well-honed hatred.) To communicate his recommendations to the television industry more easily, Nixon established the Office of Telecommunications Policy (OTP) as an arm of the executive branch.

These presidential abuses of power were revealed during the nationally televised Watergate hearings. Nixon's defenders were quick to point out that other presidents had used similar methods, and this can be documented. However, no other administration had institutionalized the process in the systematic way that Nixon chose, the same way that it is done in dictatorships. If he had not been forced to resign, he might have succeeded in tyrannizing the press with its own democratic institutions. His innovation was scope and magnitude, not method.

ACCOUNTABILITY

Will television put an incompetent in the White House? Perhaps. Some people think we already have had several. However, if a demagogue controlled television, that would be a serious problem for democracy. Although it is consoling to think that this could never happen, history has its own lessons to teach. Not long ago the government, the people, big business, the military, the press (print and electronic), and even the president were intimidated by a junior senator from Wisconsin. Only a few courageous people resisted him, and often their careers or reputations were ruined for having done so.

Consider the political implications of that famous CBS program. It was as much the handiwork of lab technicians and biased reporters as of the senator himself. Murrow and Friendly decided that he had to be stopped and so they carefully pieced together snippets of reality to make a larger-than-life collage. It was a recognizable electronic caricature in defense of democracy, as interpreted by two CBS journalists. But the same kind of thing can be done in the service of tyranny for the same purpose—to manipulate public opinion. The sword cuts both ways. Again, Nixon is an apt example.

President Nixon manipulated television with great skill, as was chronicled by Joe McGinniss's *The Selling of a President 1968*. But the book ends before the real story begins—after Nixon took office. Was it coincidence that Vice President Spiro Agnew's criticism of CBS's instant analyses of President Nixon's televised addresses, in 1973, was followed by the network's cancellation of them? Richard Salant, then president of CBS News, told a Stanford University audience in 1977 that he had no idea why the corporation's chairman, Bill Paley, ordered the analyses to stop. Salant is a lawyer by training and practice, a corporate executive, and he was a colleague of Paley's. How remarkable that he did not have the interest or curiosity to find out why his boss cut the air from these analyses.* Could it be that President Nixon put pressure on CBS, whose news department prides itself on political independence? Unthinkable? Watergate taught us that everything is thinkable.

People trust television. If the time and circumstances were right, TV could become an instrument of personal power, and a multitude of viewers could be programmed for action. Even in countries where the public knows that TV is the government's propaganda machine it is still persuasive. President de Gaulle allowed no access to TV by the opposition except during a short pre-election period when it is legally required. Everyone knew that the medium was state controlled and heavily censored. Nevertheless, when de Gaulle appeared on television, people listened: "My children, trust me." And they did, giving him their vote every time. When he appealed to their patriotism they responded, despite a strong, well-organized, and active anti-Gaullist movement whose ideas were widely read in the print media and were heard on peripheral radio stations.

Direct control is not necessary for the malicious use of TV. As McGinniss documented, Nixon manipulated the public's impression of him during his 1968 campaign despite an openly hostile press, and during his tenure the news was so skillfully managed in our media-intensive society that the United States bombed another country without the public knowing about it for eight months. This fact was an inspiration for Peter Hyams's film, *Capricorn One*, in which a Mars landing is faked by TV. Hyams admonished us to think about those months of bombing in Southeast Asia that were accompanied by a nation's ignorance: "Think of all the planes involved, all the barracks that had to be built, all the beds that had to be made, all the meals that had to be cooked," all the people who in fact *knew*, and yet Americans would not believe friendly foreign correspondents when they reported the destruction. And certainly we did not believe the enemy because they were, after all, the enemy. How could Americans trust them to know that they were being bombed? At Nuremberg, U.S. investigators asked in disbelief how German citizens could possibly have been unaware of the Nazi holocaust. More media does not mean more knowledge.

In two centuries we have not improved upon the American Founding Fathers' method for dealing with tyranny: checks and balances, divided power that is held accountable to the people who are sovereign. Whether the tyrant is an English monarch or American television, accountability is the key.

---

*In his 1977 book, *Clearing the Air,* former CBS reporter Daniel Schorr recounts a conversation between himself and Salant: "Are you convinced . . . that Paley's abolition of White House analysis was not a reaction to White House pressure?" "I'm not!" said Salant. [p. 273]

POLITICAL REALITY AND TV

Democracy in America has endured because of our willingness to adapt the political system to changing needs and values. The amendments to the Constitution reflect that willingness, that ability to say the sovereign people have made a mistake or have overlooked an important issue. This has kept democracy healthy. Today the people must face up to the problem of a television press that acts as government in some important ways and whose power cannot be exaggerated because it pervades everything. Democracy requires broadcasting to be checked and balanced through self-regulation, proliferation of press councils, pressure group activity, public access, encouraging media competition developing television archives, careful government regulation, expanding public television, and promoting analyses of TV's political power. Most important, the schools must teach electronic literacy as an antidote to passive viewing.

Perhaps a proper role for government is subsidization of TV archives, press councils, and citizens' communications groups, much the way that libraries and schools are subsidized. The government also could sponsor programs that teach viewers electronic literacy. Technological progress may eventually check TV's political power. The development and implementation of competing communication systems promise diversity, bidirectional communication, and access for those who are now excluded from the air. Democracy thrives on diversity. It is appropriate for government to provide an environment in which it can flourish.

5

PERSONALIZING POWER

INTIMACY AND POLITICAL CREDIBILITY

Television personalizes power like nothing else ever has. For the three debates between Jimmy Carter and incumbent Gerald Ford that were televised live in 1976, the average audience was 80 million people. That is one-third of our population. Four generations earlier, in 1858, during the historic debates between Abraham Lincoln and Stephen A. Douglas, audience size was limited to the speaker's voice range, about two acres. Even so, many people on the periphery tapped others on the shoulder to ask "What'd he say?" Some could not see at all because of poor eyesight, bad lighting, or simply because they were blocked by another person taller and broader than they. The old-fashioned campaign rally was social as well as political, a chance to be with neighbors and friends. But there was seldom intimacy between speaker and listener.

Television transcends space and time, encompasses vast audiences of varying interests, and yet it creates a unique atmosphere of intimacy because it is watched in people's homes where they are relaxed, their minds at ease. Through the magic of modern technology, politicians are invited guests, seen and heard clearly. Every gesture, every nuance of sound and movement is picked up by microphones and cameras to create a you-are-there feeling for each viewer. The medium works best when speakers convey the impression of being simple and direct, as if they were talking specifically to one person. That kind of televised intimacy enhances political credibility. This is what Jimmy Carter does so well. Despite a monotonous voice and unglamorous appearance, he has the powerful stage presence of a sincere and honest man. He is at home with the medium.

Carter is a modern president for whom television is a fact of political life, and he has shown considerable skill in using it to his advantage. From peanut farmer to president was not a hit-or-miss affair for the man from Plains. As Georgia's governor, he lived in Atlanta, which is part of the eastern seaboard's media establishment, and there he learned a lot about dealing with the press as a political process. This was reflected in his presidential campaign strategy. When he declared his candidacy he was relatively unknown, but by competing in many of the state primaries he got the TV coverage that he wanted and the national name recognition that goes with it. It was all part of his plan to manipulate the media, and it worked brilliantly. He won the presidency. But he found a cool reception waiting for him in his new hometown not only because he was an outsider, but also because he was a political maverick who wanted to do things his own way, regardless of established systems. As a newcomer to Washington politics, he was criticized vehemently for using the press to avoid traditional politics, for going directly to the people instead of working through their congressional representatives. In short, Carter was accused of trying to build a presidential constituency. Though his own party controlled both House and Senate, the rift between Congress and president widened as Carter used television to pursue the politics of personalized power.

Jimmy Carter is not the first chief of state to use broadcasting as an instrument of power. England's Prime Minister Winston Churchill immortalized certain moments in World War II by dramatic and successful radio appeals to his beseiged countrymen and women. Through the power of radio he fused their courage into a national will that endured "blood, sweat, toil, and tears" rather than surrender to Nazi bombing. During that same epoch, over the same BBC radio network, a relatively unknown French brigadier general, Charles de Gaulle, broadcast regularly into occupied France. His was a call to resistance against the Nazi-controlled Vichy government. At great risk, he was listened to clandestinely by Frenchwomen and men who heard him beg for their support of his self-established government in exile. At that time de Gaulle lacked territory, finances, forces, and arms. But he did have an unshakable belief in France and in his own messianic destiny as its leader. With remarkable prescience, he adapted his sonorous voice and his brilliant mind to the radio, just as he later adapted radio and then television to his own political ends.

When de Gaulle died 30 years later, Jean LaCouture described those early days: "During the essential years he was only a . . . shadow, a voice which came fabulous and foglike with the night . . . having an eloquence which blended cardinal, procurator, Latinist, and soldier." (*Le Monde*, November 11, 1970) Without exaggeration, de Gaulle's political career was launched on the airwaves, and he was a celebrated national figure long before most people knew what he looked like. As president, he took firm control of the one and only national television network to use it as an arm of power. Having little respect for politicians (de Gaulle considered himself a statesman, not a politician), he had a particular disdain for the National Assembly, which he thought was less than courageous during the war. Therefore, early in his presidential career, de Gaulle chose to talk directly to the people, via TV, instead of working his way through the political process. As the nation's patriarch he felt obliged to instruct his children—"mes enfants"—to vote for him, for France. This he did with great regularity, through televised intimacy. De Gaulle was often criticized for an arrogant use of power, but there is no doubt that he understood and mastered broadcasting, wielding it well as his personal political tool.

Here in the United States de Gaulle's contemporary, President Franklin D. Roosevelt, demonstrated similar brilliance during his famous fireside chats, which were part of radio's golden age. In those early war years, while de Gaulle's voice beamed into France, Roosevelt reassured Americans over the airwaves. The magic of the man, his strength, his leadership, his firm belief that "there is nothing to fear but fear itself," were transmitted to a listening nation. And though each family heard him separately, on their own radio receiver, they were united as a national community through the invisible bonds of broadcasting. Had Churchill and Roosevelt lived during the television age, there is little doubt that their charisma would have been equally effective on this medium.

During crises all leaders must reach down to the roots of their power, to the people. Depending on whether the government is dictatorial or benevolent, they will command the people's support with fear or trust. But without it, nothing can be done. Ironically, that necessary intimate relationship between leader and led is established today through a mass medium, a machine that makes the personal possible. Because of the intimacy that television engenders, politics now has a face and new force.

PRESIDENTIAL TELEVISION

Until recently, presidential access to television has been easy and frequent. Between 1965 and 1975, presidents have asked for air time on 45 occasions and only once was it denied.* In contrast, the Democratic congressional leadership requested access to the air 11 times in seven years (1968–1975) during Republican administrations, but received it only three times. This information comes from a study that was done at the request of former House Speaker Carl Albert, a Democrat, who asked the Congressional Research Service to prepare "A Report

---

*On October 6, 1975 CBS and NBC refused to broadcast President Gerald Ford's speech on tax cuts. See "Findings in Brief" in Congressional House of Representatives Interstate and Foreign Commerce Committee Hearings, Federal Communications Commission Oversight. March 2 and 3, 1976. P. 30.

on Simultaneous Television Network Coverage of Presidential Addresses to the Nation." According to this research, the White House, not the networks, controls presidential coverage, and the report cites certain instances when Presidents Johnson, Nixon, and Ford rallied public opinion to their points of view by appearing on TV. Having examined the data from surveys that were taken before and after presidential speeches, an eminent pollster, Louis Harris, decided that "The pattern is so consistent, with so few exceptions, that it is probably fair to conclude that Presidential use of television almost automatically gives . . . an important advantage."

Power is distributed among the three branches of government, but it is never equally divided and it is certainly not static. Constantly shifting with the force of events, the power of one branch or another enjoys primacy, although the equilibrium of all is maintained. For example, in the 1950s and 1960s the Supreme Court exercised political as well as legal power by interpreting laws liberally, which had the effect of increasing racial and sexual equality. But when the Republicans won in 1968, President Nixon used his executive powers to dominate the judicial and legislative branches of government, most notably by appointing several Supreme Court justices and by impounding funds that Congress already had allocated for specific purposes. A few years later, during the Watergate hearings, the legislative branch (and the judiciary) reasserted itself and Nixon felt the full weight of democracy's checks and balances, which culminated in his ignominious resignation.

Today it seems as if there has been a shift back toward presidential power, and some analysts believe this is because of television, which functions best when a subject is focused clearly. This is easier to do with the executive branch because a president embodies national authority, whereas Congress has over 500 representatives, fragmented leadership, and regional loyalties. But as is so often true, things are not what they seem. In reality, the executive branch has grown enormously so that its budget, personnel, agencies, departments, and complexity now challenge Congress. Nevertheless, people think of a single person, the president, when they think of the executive, whereas Congress usually conjures up two separate houses and no one leader to symbolize its power. Since the 1976 congressional report on presidential television, the commercial TV networks have been reconsidering access and the manner in which they may be manipulated by the White House.

During the first several months of Carter's presidency, there were several media events, too choice for broadcasters to ignore. First, there was the inauguration. Unquestionably newsworthy, it naturally focuses on the president. But Carter sharpened that focus by his uncanny flair for personalizing even a ritualized occasion. He captured the hearts of millions by walking hand in hand with his family to the White House on that frosty January day, instead of driving there in the presidential limousine. Shortly afterward there was a series of broadcast specials. A radio call-in allowed ordinary citizens to put questions directly to the president. The program's host was our "most trusted man in America," Walter Cronkite, whose presence gave legitimacy to the new president's promise of openness and honesty in government. Television brought us a day in the life of the president, a fireside chat about the energy crisis, a Carter tour of New England, and presidential visits to several European capitols in as many days. All of it was great copy for electronic and print journalists. But, after awhile, presidential events disappeared. Public opinion polls showed a significant decline in Carter's popularity. Television executives reported that they were rethinking presidential access to TV, and Carter's media managers debated the theory of overexposure, whose premise is that too much visibility can have a fatal effect. Although experts disagree on how much is too much, the fact is that Carter did not have the same amount or kind of TV coverage in the latter part of his first term as during his early months in office. This may reflect the networks' disenchantment with presidential access; it may reflect a White House decision to control exposure; it may be due to the realities of congressional politics, (representatives bridle at direct presidential appeals to the public, which is one way to circumvent congress) or it may be a combination of all three.

Network Disenchantment With Presidential Access

In the spring of 1977, the president's speech on energy was informally made "available for live coverage." But CBS turned it down before the two other commercial networks could respond to the offer, on the ground that it did not warrant an interruption of their programming. Shortly afterward, ABC and NBC indicated that they probably would follow suit and President Carter, for the first time since his inauguration, formally requested broadcast time on all three networks, citing national urgency as his reason. Face was saved on all sides: Carter was given access but the formal request made it clear that the networks were not mere puppets on a string. On another occasion, when White House staff made it known that President Carter would be available for a nationwide July 4 broadcast, the networks clearly were unreceptive, and nothing came of it. Another time, when Carter addressed the nation about the Panama Canal crisis, some local stations scheduled the speech for delayed broadcast. In the San Francisco area, only ABC carried it live.

The Theory of Overexposure

President Carter has been described by NBC executive Paul Klein as "a sensational performer" who "projects sincerity and truthfulness." A CBS White House correspondent, Bob Schieffer, agrees: "He says interesting things." And an expert maker of political commercials, David Garth, thinks Carter is "perfect—a quiet man in a quiet medium." (Reeves 1977)

Like most presidents since the mid-1950s, Carter has his own staff of media experts, some of whom see television as more than journalism. For them it is an entertainment medium and they are interested in giving TV what it wants: a show that will hold the audience. Others on Carter's staff are wary of show biz. They contend that if Carter acts like a TV star he will be rated like one, and eventually will be destroyed by the medium. The kind of televised specials that typified Carter's early months as president put him in the hands of the networks, enhancing their political power along with his. If this were to continue, it could lead to a power struggle between broadcasting and government.

Television takes the unknown and makes it familiar. This is what politicians think they want and need, but in the final analysis it may be detrimental to their objectives. Leadership is characterized by a mysterious quality called charisma, whose hallmark is aloofness from the masses. If television removes too many veils of mystery, it may weaken the fabric of leadership.

With increasing frequency, President Carter has used press conferences as a way of gaining access to television without engaging in network debates on the merits of that access. The conference format is such that he can start with a mini speech and, if his primary purpose is to address a particular subject, he can control the focus by limiting questions to that issue. Inasmuch as Carter had experimented with innovative television but now uses the more formal press conference, one may conclude that show biz has limited value in personalizing presidential power. In an era when commercial networks closely scrutinize and sometimes resist White House requests for air time, the press conference is a logical choice for quick and easy televised access to the public, for the media assumes that top-level press conferences deserve coverage since they usually are called in connection with newsworthy events.

The Realities of Congressional Politics

Thomas P. (Tip) O'Neill, Jr. is Carl Albert's successor as speaker of the House. A product of Boston machine politics, this rough and tumble, old-fashioned, tough, Irish politician did not back off from a political struggle between Congress and the White House. Shortly after the new president's inauguration he cautioned Carter to cooperate with Congress on legislation or risk having his own party fight him. According to O'Neill, the president told him he had handled the Georgia legislature by going over their heads, via the press, directly to the people, and when O'Neill suggested that he be careful about trying a similar tactic with Congress, Carter seemed genuinely surprised: "He didn't know what I was talking about." (Tolchin 1977) Since then, however, the president seems to have learned.

Congressional leaders were not courted, and were even ignored in the early days of Carter's administration. But after several legislative battles that the president did not win, their advice was sought and the little niceties that pay big dividends were looked to with care (for example, personal phone calls from the president to congressional leaders, invitations to the White House). When Carter publicly announced his opposition to 19 major water development projects that already had been authorized and funded by Congress, the House and Senate joined forces against him. Carter finally backed down and accepted the political realities: those projects involved jobs, contracts, and promises made. Congress had no intention of encouraging Carter to revive an imperial presidency, à la Nixon, which might run roughshod over its commitments by impounding funds or ignoring cooperation between the executive and legislative branches of government. Gradually Carter was brought around to a compromise that allowed most of the water projects to go forward, although several were set aside. Since then, Tip O'Neill has not hesitated to remind the president that governmental power is shared in this country and Congress will have its full share or fight.

American democracy is still evolving. Broadcasters resent being told what is news and what is not, especially if the telling comes from the White House. The president's staff is reining in on made-for-TV specials, and Congress has just taken a great leap forward into the twentieth century by allowing its sessions to be televised. During this struggle over television's power an old lesson in politics has reemerged: it is difficult for the chief executive to build a presidential constituency in lieu of working with Congress along traditional lines. The modern age may have produced many marvels, but the political perceptiveness of America's Founding Fathers in devising a system of checks and balances is still valid.

PUBLIC BROADCASTING AND GOVERNMENT PROPAGANDA

Someday, if commercial networks accept their civic responsibility to provide information adequate to the needs of democracy, we may have better news and public affairs programming. Meanwhile, the Public Broadcasting Service is in a position to fill a political vacuum caused by limited channels and problems with access to commercial networks.

The Carnegie Commission on the Future of Public Broadcasting concluded that PBS is an absolutely indispensable institution, meriting increased federal funds, and that commercial networks, which have free use of the public's airwaves, should contribute from their profits to its support. This sent shudders of fear through the hearts of many who believe that free enterprise should not be compelled by the government to do anything, even if it is for the public good. According to this view, the federal government has no business in the broadcasting business because government might be tempted to manipulate radio and TV for its own propaganda purposes.

The fear is real but the argument is specious. To begin with, we have few free enterprises in the United States that are not somehow regulated by the government. So broadcast regulation is not unique or inappropriate. And government always has manipulated various power sources whenever it could, from reporters to scientists, just as they, in turn, manipulate the government when they can. Fortunately, the writers of the U.S. Constitution anticipated this bit of human chicanery and allowed for it in devising our governmental process. It takes the form of interest group politics, whose power comes from the American people. The men at Philadelphia who met to form a new government were not fond of the people, but they were political realists. Although they feared the power of groups to divide national unity, they factored them into their governmental design. As for propaganda, governments everywhere engage in it. The United States is no exception. What else is the *Congressional Record* except a propaganda sheet? Despite its official-sounding name, it is not an accurate record of what happened or is said. If it were, *CR* would not publish verbatim transcripts of meetings that never took place, nor would congressional representatives be allowed to amend and edit its contents before publication. The Government Printing Office, which publishes more titles than any publishing house in America, is another great propaganda center that prints, at taxpayers' expense, various reports with definite biases, some of which do little more than propagandize political views. Taxes also pay for government press releases, electronic as well as printed, which are often incorporated into news programs and articles without identifying their source. These are circulated by government public relations experts (propagandists) to justify legions of governmental agencies and departments. Although press releases are often informational, they also are often abused to sell a program, a policy, or to manipulate opinion.

Propaganda is integral to the American political process, and it serves no one to pretend that it is not. Furthermore, it is unrealistic to think that government can be prevented much longer from using television for propaganda purposes. History shows that technology is not repressed easily. Eventually it intrudes on the most staid people and institutions. Government propaganda is far more dangerous now, disguised and distributed as press releases, than it would be if it were identified clearly as such. It might be better if the government had regularly scheduled access to PBS to present its views and to have them so labeled. After all, every report is biased so bias is not the problem. The problem is to know what the bias is. Then one can properly analyze the information, according to its source.

Competing ideas characterize a free society. America's challenge is not to eliminate government propaganda. That is an unrealistic goal. Wherever there are institutions there will be propagandists employed to promote their interests, whether they are private or governmental. But the people can decide whether to integrate or isolate propaganda, to call it by its name or pretend that it does not exist.

In a modern democratic society government representatives should have easy access to the people and the people should be able to hear their representatives, especially over airwaves that belong to them and for which they ultimately pay through traditional and hidden taxes. This right to hear as well as to be heard is a part of free speech that is guaranteed by the First Amendment. Broadcasters have no authority to abridge that freedom by denying the people or their representatives reasonable access to the air. Obviously, they have conceded the point because they now allow free speech messages that express listeners' views, and there is an industrywide trend that encourages audience input. This, too, is a personalization of power. The faceless, voiceless masses are finally exercising their right to be heard as well as to hear.

Broadcasters always have treated television as if the free press would be sullied should anyone have access to TV whom they did not invite or for whom they had not decided to grant a request for air time. Therefore, industry executives believe they must control the public's airwaves. Said differently, broadcasters have decided that big business (remember, television is big business for it ranks along with other large multinationals) should control the public's interest, although this is and always has been a governmental function. It is, in fact, the reason why governments were formed in the first place. The television industry's desire to maintain the status quo is understandable because power is seldom relinquished with good cheer. But the people have a right to considerable power over how their airwaves and how the taxes that they pay on TV-advertised products are used. The TV industry has no reason to fear. A paradox of freedom is that, like love, it becomes stronger as it is shared. Opening the channels of communication to the people and their representatives will have a strengthening effect on democracy.

PEOPLE POWER

Television not only affords access to authority figures and the institutions they represent, it also helps people to communicate with one another, and this affirms their validity. Once that is accomplished, the dynamics of self-respect sometimes gives people enough courage to ask for improvements in their quality of life, or for participation in the decision-making process itself.

When people with similar problems meet and share their experiences, there is a consciousness raising that may produce unforeseen political power. This was clearly the case in the 1950s when a group of Congolese tribal chiefs were brought to Brussels in connection with a World's Fair exposition. It was the first time they had met as a group and they used the occasion to plot a revolution against their mother country, Belgium, for exploiting their resources and people. According to Colin Legum's analysis, it is unlikely that such a meeting would have taken place in the Congo itself since the chiefs were separated by natural boundaries such as rivers and jungles. Also, the the politics of colonial life did not encourage such meetings precisely because communication can be a prelude to political action. (Legum 1961)

Once people have access to information that encourages their belief in certain goals, it may be hard to stop them from trying to reach those goals because credibility is the keystone of power. Before the uprising, Belgium suppressed information in the Congo about the decolonization that was taking place in other parts of Africa. However, when the tribal chiefs met and exchanged the bits and pieces of information that each had about what was happening elsewhere, they saw an encouraging pattern: many Africans had overcome seemingly insurmountable odds and European colonizers were being forced out. If rebellion could bring national independence to others, then it might bring it to the Congo.

Today, Americans do not need an international exposition to bring together leaders or members of various subgroups. Television does that. Initially, televised "meetings" took the form of news coverage. Demonstrations in one part of the country were broadcast nationally and a responsive chord was struck. It created a meeting of hearts and minds among formerly isolated groups. Viewers learned that others with similar problems had arrived successfully at solutions or challenged authorities as a result of certain tactics. In this way television became teacher and advocate. People power was no longer an abstract newspaper account. Nor was it merely a faceless radio voice. It personalized the power of ordinary people who took action to achieve their ends. For instance, American Indians were stupefied to see the television reports of chaos that radical Indians had caused when they ransacked the Bureau of Indian Affairs building in the nation's capitol during the early 1970s. Afterward, government representatives invited the press to photograph and televise the extensive vandalism. That decision was two-edged. While it did encourage anti-Indian sentiment among some viewers, which is what the government intended, it also taught formerly passive Indians that violence is an effective way to get attention. That kind of lesson is not lost on other disadvantaged groups. In situations like this, television unwittingly becomes an advocate of violence, partly because the events that TV selects to report as news are violent, and partly because television executives insist on action shots, which is the industry euphemism for pictures showing violence.

The relationship of television news coverage to the shape and tone of society is another of those immeasurables whose impact cannot be denied. Particularly in the last generation, while TV was becoming our most dominant means of communication, there has been a redistribution of power in the United States. People have learned from one another, via television, that they have real power, once they are organized and in front of the cameras. Rebellious citizens against the U.S.-Indochina war influenced President Johnson's decision not to run again in 1968; they were also a decisive factor in America's eventual withdrawal from Southeast Asia. Protesting minorities have forced social, political, economic, and legal changes in all sectors of society. Progress is inadequate but it holds promise. In almost every instance the changes have been spurred, if not catalyzed, by media coverage. The effect is cyclical: televised news makes it clear that ordinary people (including minorities, women, the aged, the young, and the handicapped) can be quite capable, that they are not necessarily social derelicts or wild-eyed radicals. This affects the way these people are portrayed in other TV programs, because art does imitate life, which, in turn, affects viewer attitudes, encouraging similar activist behavior and increasing tolerance or resentment. Then those attitudes and behavior affect authority, order, community, credibility, and the way they are expressed in institutions.

One deeply held modern myth is that technology leads to standardization, depersonalization, mass mentality, and alienation. The facts themselves do not support this, except as a transitional phenomenon. What is true about mass production is also true about the mass media. For example, Volkswagen began producing "the people's car" in Germany during the 1930s. At that time it was as standardized as shoelace holes: one size, one format, one color—black. After World War II, production increased and the bug, as it was called, established an enviable record for durability, reliability, and economy. Many countries were importing it, and it sold well everywhere despite the absence of variations on a theme. Then, after some years, there was a startling change, as if the little black bugs were falling into an artist's palette. They rolled off assembly lines like brightly colored Easter eggs in burnt orange, daffodil yellow, coral red, sea blue, and every imaginable hue of color. Standardization gave way to options at additional cost: sun roofs, convertible tops, whitewall tires, spoked wheels, and a range of other features. The variety was a logical consequence of technological development.

The Volkswagen example is not an exception. Similar diversification is found in the products of other technologies. The process is first, an initial stage of standardization with no deviation; then, somewhat later, an explosion of differences. Shoes are a good example, especially women's shoes. They come in a multitude of fabrics, colors, and styles, so that it is difficult to imagine a nation of women's feet all shod in the same way, such as one found in China during the 1940s when its shoe production did not include much variation. Here in the United States, when technology first provided us with machine-made shoes, we had similar uniformity. The range of choice was from A to B. Essentially, all one needed to know was size. Now, the selection possibilities are dazzling and the size is often the last thing a salesperson inquires about.

The point is that technology has provided us with a vast array of information sources that will continue to expand as our methods for communicating expand. A simplistic fear is that we will all end up thinking alike because we are exposed to the mass media. But the mass media are not a monolith. Now that print is as common as grass, we have an enormous assortment of specialty magazines, journals, newspapers, and books that appeal to a honeycomb of subcultures comprising society. Skateboard enthusiasts have their own magazines, as do cultists, sailors, gamblers, homosexuals, religious and political extremists, children, working mothers, dog lovers, scholars, crossword puzzle devotees, business tycoons, small investors, health specialists, and soothsayers. Whatever the subject, someone is publishing at least a newsletter about it. We will eventually have the same kind of experience in video communication. Future technology will provide thousands of channels from which to choose programs that meet special interests. Now, however, TV is in a holding pattern, with only three national commercial networks and one national public network. Since there is little difference in the subject or quality of commercial programming, there is definitely a mass aspect to it. But the situation is temporary. Broadcasting in the United States is already in the throes of change: the combination of satellite and cable technology TV (just to consider one example) has brought the consumer a multiplicity of channels, some national in scope.

As people have more access to communication systems, they can have a greater impact on society than was possible in the past, if only because they now command a national audience. Change itself is not the distinguishing hallmark of today. What is different is the speed with which things happen, the number of people who can learn about them instantly and simultaneously, and the scope of effects, which can be global.

Although it is fashionable, it is inaccurate to say that contemporary America lacks leaders, individuality, and moral fiber. Society is more complex now than it was in the eighteenth century when democracy in America came on the scene, and government's responsibilities are greater, at home as well as abroad. Nevertheless, more people are politically active today than in the past. More individuality is possible because there is more opportunity to express it. Millions still work at monotonous tasks, in wretched conditions, but they work fewer hours (about one-third fewer) than their grandparents and they have more possibilities to use their leisure time creatively. The United States still has the poor, the sick, the slums, the inequities that need to be corrected. But in many ways the quality of life is better. Contemporary Americans have a sense of community that is deeper and more encompassing. This is due largely to communication systems, predominantly television, which have broadened and personalized the base of democracy.

6

WATERGATE: A NATIONAL CIVICS LESSON

PRECEDENT

The Senate's televised Watergate hearings were a national civics lesson, a morality play that was broadcast here and abroad for several weeks in 1973. Scene by scene, a tale was told of how the mighty had fallen. It was a compelling story of strength and terrible weakness, of ineluctable forces playing upon the flawed character of men who lusted for power and used it unwisely.

Richard Nixon's abuse of presidential power was not unique in the annals of American democracy. Nor was his hostility to the press. That relationship is traditionally an adversary one and political health requires it to be that way. Journalists see themselves as guardians of the public's interest, whereas presidents often see them as fault-finding intruders who file irresponsible reports. Like Nixon, several presidents have tried to control or influence the press and to harass or punish their opponents. Franklin Roosevelt used the FBI to compile dossiers of people who sent telegrams to the White House supporting Charles Lindbergh's criticism of Roosevelt's foreign policy. He also asked the FBI to wiretap some of his aides' telephones. President Eisenhower is reported to have asked the FBI for information about southern governors and congressmen who opposed his racial integration policies. Attorney General Robert Kennedy authorized an FBI wiretap on black leader Martin Luther King. And President Johnson allegedly asked the FBI to investigate several journalists. This information was widely publicized as a spillover effect of the Watergate investigations. (Royster 1975; Wise 1976; Lasky 1977)

A NATIONAL CIVICS LESSON

Despite precedent, Nixon's abuse of power was unique for its scope and intensity, for his efforts to institutionalize government control of the media, for the disclosure of his illegal acts to the nation by his own aides while he was still president, and for his self-indictment on White House tape recordings that he secretly made but never intended for public release. The making and keeping of those tapes were an unparalleled act of political folly. It is almost inconceivable that a president would sit in the oval office, using language that would make a sailor blush, planning tactics that would make Machiavelli look like a political amateur, and sound as if he were unaware of a voice-activated recording system that was installed at his request. There are many reasons to believe that Nixon had poor judgment, but this is one of the best.

Because of the televised Watergate hearings, millions of people in several countries sat in judgment on an American president for the first time in history. What they saw was a dramatization of the U.S. political process, the constitutional checks and balances at work. It was an affirmation of the democratic principle that no one is above the law (although many people feel the law was lenient with Nixon and that he should have been tried as a criminal). Daniel Boorstin, an eminent historian who writes about American democracy, puts it this way: ". . . one of the curious problems of democracy . . . is the result of the development of the electronic media . . . we used to think of the conscience as being a private, intimate, still, small voice within. Now the conscience of democracy becomes the whole community sitting in the living room watching what has been done." (Congressional Quarterly, *Watergate: Chronology of a Crisis*, vol. 1)

During that spring and summer of 1973, television provided a national platform for a discussion of political theory, particularly the use of power in a democracy. It was done with all the seriousness that professionals could bring to the subject. Yet the proceedings were followed avidly despite long stretches of tedium. Perhaps the viewers' staying power is best explained by the fact that Watergate became an allegory. It can be interpreted on many levels, according to one's knowledge and experience. For some people it is only a bungled Republican break-in of the Democrats' presidential campaign headquarters at the Watergate building in downtown Washington, D.C. Others see it as an exercise in poor judgment, nothing more: boys-as-men, playing at political espionage, using burglary, intrigue, graft, extortion, wiretaps, lies, coverups, harassment, surveillance, and character assassination to win a presidential election for the Republicans. Or Watergate may be seen as an ethical problem, an attempt to justify the use of any means to achieve an end. One could extend this last interpretation to say it was symptomatic of a diseased democracy. But the rejoinder to this charge is that the Watergate break-in and investigations tested the essence of American democracy and found it working well: separated powers, checked and balanced. Through the drama of Watergate Americans learned again to value vigilance as the price of freedom. Television helped to restore public respect for Congress, which had occupied a less visible place in government as TV grew and focused on the presidency. The congressional decision to press for a complete investigation of Watergate, even if it meant impeaching the president, was admirable. Similarly, the integrity of the courts system was dramatized. Judge John Sirica's courage during the criminal prosecution of the break-in was an important factor in arriving at the extraordinary political motives behind a seemingly common crime. The overall dynamics of Watergate illustrate once again the wisdom of America's Founding Fathers.

TELEVISED COVERAGE

After the first two weeks of Watergate coverage, the commercial networks responded to some viewer's complaints and rotated the Senate's hearings among themselves so that their schedules were interrupted only every third day that the hearings were in session. Public television continued taping the proceedings from gavel to gavel and ran the coverage at night, much to the gratitude of millions who were unable to follow them live. Network executives were surprised that the audience for Watergate compared favorably with Nielsen ratings for daytime programming, which are mostly soap operas (so-called because soap manufacturers were the principal advertisers for daytime TV and radio love stories). It is surmised that the makeup of the daily audience changed radically during Watergate. Many people who seldom watched TV during the day had rearranged their schedules so that they could follow the hearings. Network representatives noted that the station covering the hearings on any particular day soared the highest in audience ratings during the time that they were broadcast. In the first week the Senate's investigation was received in more than 47 million homes. Assuming that there were 1.5 viewers per set, that would mean nearly 70 million people followed the proceedings. Through technological innovation the Senate's chambers were extended to a cross section of ordinary citizens, from children who followed Watergate as part of their school assignment, to public opinon leaders, to TV addicts who watch anything.

In many respects the Senate's Watergate hearings were among the finest hours in commercial television's history. Daytime coverage averaged five hours, and it has been estimated that network production costs ran close to $100,000 daily. This public service programming was provided by the networks despite a loss of advertising revenue that CBS has described as "considerable," though the dollar terms were not spelled out precisely. Despite numerous complaints from viewers who resented even rotating coverage, because it interfered with their favorite programs, the networks held fast and pursued the big story. As the hearings progressed throughout late spring and summer, the networks accommodated their financial needs by plugging in commercials as they normally would do for any other program. Still, they deserve all the credit that they have received for recognizing the social and political importance of Watergate.

As for public broadcasting, their representatives seem to agree that the hearings put them on the map for their complete, delayed coverage. Quite rightly, they take pride in being broadcasting's "book" of public record with respect to Watergate. Unfortunately, it is not a book to which the public has access because public TV is even more poorly organized than commercial television when it comes to maintaining archives of video history and providing research opportunities for their use.

AUTHORITY AND CREDIBILITY

All governments, whether autocratic or democratic, are faced with the problems of authority, order, community, and credibility. Who is to have authority and how should it be exercised? Is national community strong enough to withstand civil disturbances? How should order be maintained or restored? And can the government's credibility endure? These central themes of political theory were examined carefully, in the American context, during the Watergate hearings.

For the past 20 years televised political authority has tended to crystallize in the person of the president, largely because TV works especially well when the subject matter allows a sharp focus. And it is easy, if erroneous, to think the president embodies national power because the legislative and judicial branches of government are fragmented among regional representatives: hundreds in the House and Senate and thousands in the courts. Therefore, the president has come to symbolize authority in TV's version of America, and presidential prestige is enhanced by the medium's high credibility ratings. In political terms, this means presidents wield extraordinary power because they are trusted and believed, which is why shockwaves went through the nation when Watergate revealed illegal practices in other administrations, as well as in Richard Nixon's. The public's astonishment was directly related to its naiveté about political affairs, which persists despite numerous opportunities to become knowledgeable. But, as George Santayana observed, those who are unwilling to learn the lessons of history are doomed to repeat them.

In the early 1960s, highly credentialed journalists passively accepted presidential accounts of the U.S. war in Vietnam and duly reported the misinformation for public consumption partly because the president said it was true. This might be understandable if it were the first time that a president had lied publicly, but it was not.

Americans learned about presidential lying in May 1960 when Francis Gary Powers, a U-2 pilot, was shot down and taken prisoner 1,200 miles inside of the Soviet Union. The U.S. government did not know that he had survived the crash or that he had not pushed the destruct button before bailing out. When the Soviet Union accused the United States of aerial spying, the State Department vehemently denied it. However, President Eisenhower had approved the development of the U-2, and he knew that flights had been occurring for four years to gather information about Soviet strategic missiles. Since the Soviet Union and the United States were technically at peace, it would have been indelicate to be caught spying. And so the president was enormously embarrassed when the Soviet Union produced Powers and paraded him before the Moscow press corps. In addition to Powers's confession, the Soviets had retrieved enough of the plane to verify its mission. For politically knowledgeable people this incident was not extraordinary. It was reality politics. All nations collect information about their real, imagined, and potential enemies. The United States may call it aerial reconnaissance, data gathering, or whatever, but traditionally it is called spying. However, the U-2 incident was not taken in stride by ordinary citizens. Ike was a war hero. He was admired as a good and honest man. He was president of the United States. Would he lie to his own people? It was unheard of. And yet, on May 9, President Eisenhower finally told the world that Powers was spying.

Did the public learn from this experience? Not really. People drifted right back into a trusting mode, and two years later when President Kennedy told the nation that U.S. military forces in Vietnam were advisors, people believed him. Worse still, American journalists believed him. No one dared to say that the handsome young president with the beautiful wife and the spirit of Camelot image was manipulating the press and the public. Kennedy's charm had cast a veil over reporters' minds. A legend was in the making and few journalists had the professionalism to follow their common sense to its inevitable conclusion: the president lied.

President Johnson, Kennedy's successor, also lied. It was the path of least resistance. The public was docile and accepting. Most of its self-appointed watchdogs were fast asleep while presidential directives entrenched an American army in South Vietnam, tacitly approved the assassination of its president, Ngo Dinh Diem, and publicly insisted that our role was advisory. That labyrinth of lies began with Kennedy and was sustained through three administrations until Nixon resigned in 1974, nearly a dozen years later.

"NEWS MANAGEMENT"

How can these things happen in an open society where there is a free flow of information? How could the press be taken in so completely over such a long period of time? Like many things, the explanation ties into U.S. history. The roots of America's heritage are religious, and, ironically, that is a partial reason for cloaking foreign policy in morality. Like our forebears, who were good puritans, policymakers want to purify U.S. actions by lofty motives. When the United States went to war against the Nazis it was to aid American allies, not because the U.S. might be next on Germany's list. When American troops went to South Vietnam it was to protect that part of the world from godless communism, to make it safe for democracy, and not because America wanted to protect its sphere of influence in Southeast Asia.

The United States is not much different from other countries in this respect. A war effort cannot be sustained unless the public is mobilized to support it. This is done most easily if some high-sounding reason (ideology) is found to rationalize increasing taxes, working more, getting less, and the deaths of hundreds of thousands. The problem is that this approach requires a great deal of image-making and, after awhile, it is increasingly easy to confuse image with reality. One becomes adept at dealing with appearances. Then, when a crisis is past, the precedents of intrigue and deception remain.

Although TV executives argue that they are exposed to more governmental pressure than other media because their stations are licensed by the government, this is probably exaggerated. Presidents, their staffs and government representatives from the legislature and from many different agencies have tried to bring similar pressure on newspapers. Columnist Mary McGrory was on President Nixon's enemies' list, as was Katharine Graham, publisher of the *Washington Post*. Politicians are sensitive about their public image and they will have suggestions and criticisms of the press regardless of whether the government licenses the medium. Trying to influence others' thoughts and behavior is simply a fact of life that expresses itself as pressure politics. It may not be the most attractive feature of American government but there is nothing to be gained by denying its existence.

An interesting phenomenon is that television makes certain kinds of news management extremely risky. When manipulation is reported on television, as was done with Watergate, it is on a global scale, instantly and simultaneously. The effects can be devastating. Perhaps this has and will continue to have a salutary political effect.

HONESTY IN GOVERNMENT

Watergate was a political coming of age for many people who watched the proceedings on television. It was like losing one's innocence to learn that the president, his aides, and the country's chief law enforcement officer, Attorney General John Mitchell, had sanctioned criminal acts. Even more surprising and frightening were their selfless motives. No one sought personal gain. They believed it was in the nation's best interests for Nixon to be re-elected and that illegal acts were acceptable to accomplish that end. This attitude permeated the presidency. Even after his resignation, Nixon reaffirmed it on national television when he was interviewed by David Frost. Apparently he did not learn Watergate's lesson: despite a flawed political system all power in American democracy is accountable to the people.

One of the great mysteries about democracy is that it functions at all: corruption and ouright ignorance can be found at all levels of government and among the people themselves; many Americans have no interest in politics; others do not understand the issues; some are unbelievably biased. And yet the system works. The United States has had a stable form of government for two centuries. Perhaps the explanation is that wherever there are people there are imperfections, but, on balance, there is a preponderence of honesty and intelligence everywhere. During the Watergate era there was a lot of talk about how politicians basically are dishonest because politics is a depraved environment that attracts immoral people. This is a popular and commonly held opinion, but it is wrong. Politics is no more corrupt than other human institutions, including great universities and churches. Corruption is expressed in different ways. University graft may take the form of admitting unqualified applicants whose parents are important benefactors, or taking tuition money from students who major in fields for which there are few positions after graduation, or in administrators who persist in sexual and racial discrimination despite laws to the contrary. Religion has a long history of corruption that spans the full range of depravation: inquisitions, torture, human sacrifices, and financial extortion are just a few examples. In short, politicians have not cornered the market on corruption. There is enough to go around for every sector of society in every country of the world.

And yet, these facts do not support a philosophy of despair. There are fine educators and religious leaders. Many people benefit from both education and religion. Similarly, there is more freedom and equality under the law for more Americans today than there was in the eighteenth century. More people participate in the political process now than in the past, even though fewer go to the polls. For every corrupt politician there are thousands of honest women and men who work as elected, appointed, or volunteer officials. Some of them must be doing something right. Since 1946 the United States has avoided a world war despite regional wars that could have escalated into global conflicts. The use of nuclear arms has been avoided although the technology is there and the temptation has been great. In terms of education and social services, the quality of life has never been better. Professionals, from business executives to doctors, are being forced to think of the public's interest and to adjust their performance accordingly. It is easy to romanticize the past, but the present is not without merit in spite of major problems.

Daniel Boorstin, an authority on American democracy, believes that "The quality of people in politics today is as high as it ever was" in all three branches of government. He made this assessment shortly after Watergate. Governments come and go but human nature remains much the same. Power will continue to attract the usual mix of moral character. While it is true that Nixon's administration had more than its share of fainthearted men, it is also true that their contemporaries in Congress and in the courts had, and exercised, tremendous moral courage and fortitude in bringing them to justice. And it was done openly for the world to see. Do we need to look further than Senator Sam Ervin, chairman of the Watergate committee, or Judge John Sirica, who heard the Watergate criminal case, to find examples of superb leadership and impeccable moral fiber?

Today life is complex and demanding. The pace is faster, the ramifications of actions are more immediate and extensive. But most of the time the voters find people who measure up to the demands that are made upon them. Past leaders also have had frailties. Corruption did not start with Watergate and it is not confined to government.

The televised Senate Watergate hearings were a massive politicizing process. They unfolded in real time (as and when they actually took place, except for the PBS delayed broadcast which was, however, uncut) and they were the talk of the country. Day after day, through a spring and summer, people shared not only what they had seen and heard, but how they interpreted the testimony and what they thought might happen next. Viewers who had not considered the Constitution since they finished high school were getting a step-by-step review of American political theory. For many of them it was the most thrilling political experience of their lives. It blended disillusionment and unabashed admiration for the daring courage that unraveled a skein of high-level corruption under the glare of television lights in the presence of reporters from many countries. It was a democratic event in the most profound sense of the word because television brought together millions of people from all different backgrounds to share a national crisis. It was political participation at a deeply felt level. One may argue that the attraction was perversion, not politics, that the audience was drawn by a sadistic pleasure in the discomfort of others. But the drama lay in ideas, not action. Watergate was not an easy exercise in viewership. It required a commitment to follow the labyrinth of facts, and laying them out was often an exercise in tedium. For every witticism or shocking revelation there hours of bare-bones testimony, devoid of humor or sensation.

People may never know precisely whether the Watergate hearings politicized viewers who were usually indifferent to politics. What is known is that 47 million homes tuned into the televised proceedings the first week and while that may indicate many things, it does not indicate political apathy.

7

BROADCASTING ENTERS AN ERA OF PUBLIC ACCOUNTABILITY

ACCESS AND ACCOUNTABILITY

Until 1968, television news executives engaged in a subtle form of censorship about which little was known and less was said. It resulted from an industrywide practice of erasing videotapes, which were not only costly but also took a great deal of storage space, so that they could be reused. The first 20 years of American TV news-as-broadcast was destroyed with the blessing of managers who either had no sense of history or who had the political astuteness to realize that an absence of records increases power.

Since the dawn of history people have been preoccupied with recording and circulating tribal, religious, national, economic, political, and social mores. How remarkable, therefore, that well-educated, modern, professional communicators would allow a generation of video history to vanish despite the medium's power and influence in our culture. Although each network wanted nothing more than to have the maximum number of viewers see its version of the evening news from 7:00 to 7:30, all of them wanted nothing less than to provide public access to that same news at 7:31 or thereafter. Although many analysts have thought deeply about television's political role in America, few have turned their attention to the fact that broadcasters exercised their power while luxuriating in the absence of public accountability. This situation is being remedied gradually by the new phenomenon of television news archives, which is as important to electronic democracy as was the establishment of public library and school systems in the linear era.

In 1968, Paul Simpson—lawyer, news buff, political independent, retired insurance executive—challenged the networks' policy of nonaccess and their historic insensitivity. He persuaded his alma mater, Vanderbilt University, to house an archive of commercial network evening news as it was taped off the air in Nashville, Tennessee. This collection, which he initially funded, has become the highly respected Television News Archive (TNA). It is a nonprofit, nonpartisan, privately financed institution whose collection is available to everyone, here and abroad. Its policies are simple, practical, and user oriented. Like libraries, it lends materials. (There is a reasonable fee which, however, does not begin to meet the Archive's expenses.) It has been rumored in TV circles that TNA was founded as an instrument of the Nixon administration to persecute the networks, à la Agnew, but this is patently absurd. TNA was founded in the summer of 1968 and Nixon was not elected until November of that year. Furthermore, the Archive's resources have been borrowed by some users to defend the networks against charges that they were anti-Nixon.

Simpson apprised the networks of his archive, and there was no negative feedback until December 1973 when CBS sued TNA for infringing its copyright on "CBS Evening News with Walter Cronkite," which the network registered with the copyright office in April 1973 as an "unpublished motion picture other than a photoplay." A later revision changed the wording to "a published motion picture." When the Copyright Act was recently revised, TNA's activities were "grandfathered" in (protected under the new law), and CBS dropped its suit, which had brought the network nothing but criticism in the print media for trying to impede freedom of information. Since then television archives have been proliferating and several are in gestation.

TELEVISION NEWS ARCHIVES

A few of the better known archives, beside the Vanderbilt University Television News Archive in Nashville, are the Television News Study Center at George Washington University Library in Washington, D.C., which enlarges access to Vanderbilt's archive; CBS's News Archive and the Museum of Broadcasting, both in New York City; the National Archives' Audiovisual Division, the Library of Congress's Motion Picture and Recorded Sound Division, and the National Academy of Television Arts and Sciences' archives, which are housed in the University of California at Los Angeles' Film and TV Archive.

In addition to the archives, TV archivists' associations have come into being, most notably the International Studies Association at Kansas State University; the TV Archives Advisory Committee, a consensus organization, which was hosted by the Library of Congress in 1978; the International Federation of Television Archives, known as FIAT, which includes broadcasting companies from France, England, Germany, Italy, Japan, Canada, Netherlands, Turkey, Spain, Brazil, Iran, and the United States.

Vanderbilt Television News Archive

This collection includes the commercial networks weekday evening news from August 5, 1968 to the present; special news events such as Nixon's resignation and farewell address, presidential speeches and press conferences, the Watergate hearings, the Ford-Carter debates; public affairs programs, such as interviews from "Face the Nation," "Issues and Answers," and "Meet the Press."

TNA has an index and abstracts dating from 1968, (the *Television News Index and Abstracts*). With it as a guide, users make editorial judgments, specifying which segments or programs they would like to use. If there is a particular subject that interests them, the specific news segments are indicated on an order form and are spliced together by the archive to make a compiled subject tape. However, TNA will not do this if users simply say "I want the news about Wounded Knee." The actual selection (that is, the editorial decisions) is the users' responsibility. If the materials are being requested by mail instead of being used on site, TNA will request a deposit, a user fee, and a signed promise not to duplicate or have a public showing of the tape without permission. As CBS pointed out during the course of their lawsuit against TNA, there is no guarantee that these promises will be kept. The Archive's answer is that this is a risk one takes in a free society that relies on an informed citizenry to preserve democracy.

Tapes are mailed directly to the person who has requested them, which simplifies research since one is not reliant on the local library for a playback machine or restricted to the library's hours. Another advantage is that when a tape goes directly to the user, it may be integrated into classroom work, which is not a public showing, to teach electronic literacy or as an important analytical tool in various courses.

Television News Study Center

The Center, situated at the George Washington University Library in Washington, D.C., opened in the fall of 1978. It is not an archive as it does not have its own collection of newscasts, but it provides access to the Vanderbilt Television News Archive by providing reference services and playback facilities for use of TNA sources by people who are doing research in the Washington, D.C. area. Other reference and referral services are provided to TV materials at the National Archives, the CBS News Archives, and the Museum of Broadcasting. The Center also does the taping of weekend network news and specials, which are added to the Vanderbilt Archive.

The Library of Congress Motion Picture and Recorded Sound Division

The Library of Congress's (LC) television archive is in gestation. It will house a wide spectrum of programming, including public affairs and news. One idea under discussion is for the Library to tape off the air whatever is broadcast in prime time, between 7:00 p.m. and 11:00 p.m. In addition, their collection will continue to include published programs that are deposited for copyright protection. Under the new copyright law,"published"is interpreted to encompass all programs that are distributed through sale, loan, rentals, or agreement to sell, lend, or rent. This means the collection will be quite extensive and it may include more than copyrighted news programs. Access policies have not yet been determined. Obviously, this will be an important video resource, especially if the lending policy is user oriented. But if the LC decides against making compiled subject tapes, they will, effectively, deny access just as CBS and the National Archives do. In that case their video resources will not be stored, they will be entombed. The politics of compiling subject tapes will be discussed further, below.

National Archives, Audiovisual Archives Division

An example of entombment can be had at the National Archives (NA) Audiovisual Division, a few blocks away from the Library of Congress in Washington, D.C. They accepted CBS's prohibition of compiled tapes in exchange for CBS making its hard news (morning, noon, evening, and specials) and some public affairs programming available as gifts. ABC's and NBC's agreements with NA allow the Department of Defense to tape their evening news off the air for the NA. Materials may be borrowed through the mail from NA, under the terms of interlibrary loan agreements, but they are mailed from institution to institution, not to the user. This means that one's research will be done at the convenience of the library and that if one's local library does not have a playback facility, it may be necessary to travel to the next library or the next because there is no provision for lending on an institution-to-person basis. Therefore, even if the researcher has access to a playback machine in an office, it cannot be used.

A spillover effect of the institution-to-institution policy is that the National Archives resources may not be used for teaching. This is a great loss to education, especially since there is an urgent need for instruction in electronic literacy. However, for those who can work at the National Archives during its business hours, this resource offers the distinctive feature of multimedia research: in addition to television there is easy access to films, still photographs, audio-only tapes, recordings, and printed matter. Therefore, on-site research possibilities are considerable. And, what is important for the future, NA is reprocessing its collection so that it is truly of archival quality.

A word in passing, with respect to compiled tapes. The National Archives policy is a clear example of an institution being a prisoner of its past. If the Archives does not compile material from print, they why should it compile video-material? The answer is, of course, that they are two quite different media, from two distinctly different ages of communication: the linear and the electronic. It is incumbent on institutions to move with the times if they are not to fall into disuse and atrophy. New technology requires new policy.

The Museum of Broadcasting, New York City

MB's user policies are as much a part of the nineteenth century as are the policies of the National Archives. This is not surprising since they were both formulated by CBS, which is responsible for the mandate against compiled tapes. Therefore, this source also denies access and severely limits use for educational purposes.

The collection itself is an exciting one. It houses a selection of 50 years of broadcasting about political, cultural, and social Americana. This museum is the product of William Paley's concern and personal generosity. As chairman of the board of CBS, he was aware that there was no record of significant televised events available to the public. (He was not only aware, he also must have been the reason why TV news was destroyed. As chief of CBS itself—the News Division is merely one facet of CBS, the multinational corporation—Paley was a key decision maker in CBS news policy.) Unlike the Vanderbilt Television News Archive these resources may be used only on site. It is, however, an impressive facility that includes eight playback consoles. Each accommodates three viewers, and the entire room can be wired into the same program for the benefit of groups that are not larger than 24 people. It is unfortunate that MB has opted for this functional limitation on instructional possibilities, especially in a city qhere shepherding a class of children from, say, the Bronx to central New York, where MB is located, is an undertaking of heroic proportions. Although this heroism occurs frequently so that children can hear the symphony or see the zoo, that is because orchestras and elephants will not fit easily into mailboxes or classrooms. But videotapes do. Perhaps the museum will develop more user-oriented policies in the future. Nonetheless, the museum is a step in the right direction. One terrific advantage to using it is that it has a computerized and a manual card index, with as many as 15 cross-references according to subject, title, date, producer, director, acting, and technical credits. If the index were combined with twentieth-century user policies, the museum would, indeed, be organized for access.

CBS News Archives

Having started as the Information Department for the CBS News Division, the Archives contain films, videotapes, audiotapes, and transcripts from CBS TV and radio news broadcasts, as well as from public affairs programming. In 1974 CBS began keeping videotapes of their entire newscasts. Before that time, as far back as 1960, only film and tapes that were judged of historic value were kept. CBS also has a collection of audiotapes of entire newscasts that go back to 1950, but the collection is not complete. Transcripts of televised news go back to 1967 or 1966; earlier programs have only the sketchiest of notes on their contents.*
Film segments and outtakes are also available for the same time period (1950–present) and are filed under subject for use as stock footage or for sale. CBS also has an excellent collection of documentaries, including "CBS Reports," "CBS News Specials," "CBS Special Reports," "60 Minutes," "Face the Nation," "In the News" and "30 Minutes." Since this facility is primarily for in-house use, CBS is not prepared to meet the public's need for access to television programs. Nonetheless, it is reported to have sent out 3,400 transcripts and excerpts to viewers who requested them in 1975. (Benard 1976)

Of the three networks, CBS is the most forward looking and has taken an industry leadership role in the field of TV archives. Another way of saying this is that the entire broadcasting industry works in a twentieth-century field that is guided by medieval policies about the free flow of information. NBC is taking some steps toward a better organized archive to put theirs on a more professional footing. ABC seems to be less aware of how important television archives are. The two networks took a wait-and-see attitude, letting CBS carry the burden of litigation against Vanderbilt University's Television News Archive. They followed along when CBS established a liaison with the National Archives in Washington, D.C. (but they are not as generous as CBS when it comes to providing material). In many ways it is unfortunate that CBS is subject to so much criticism because theirs is the most enlightened archival policy of the three networks (public television is still in the dark ages). However, one price of leadership is that people assess your decisions. Among the networks, CBS is on point, with respect to access policy, and therefore their decisions are evaluated constantly. However, the outstanding model for TV archives is still Vanderbilt University's Television News Archive.

CBS uses a computerized information retrieval system for materials dating from 1971 and it prepared the *CBS News Index* and *CBS News Television Broadcasts* (index and transcripts since 1975). It forbids the compilation of subject tapes, which means that despite its computer and use of video cassettes, their policy effectively denies access to information.

---

*As confirmed by CBS archivist S. Suratt to author, March 19, 1974.

American Television Arts and Sciences-University of California at Los Angeles TV Archives (ATAS-UCLA)

This is an on-site facility, housing programs from 1948 to the present. Several thousand programs have been catalogued, but several thousand more are not yet catalogued. Special arrangements can be made with the director to borrow material for classroom use, but that is discouraged since the material is not in video cassette format. This collection does not include news programs, except for a dozen or so local shows and some clips of news interviews.

Public Broadcasting Service

Public Broadcasting Service would like to develop an archive and it will if it receives funding. Meanwhile, it has a small grant from the Corporation for Public Broadcasting, which allows it to say that it has an "archives project." The Public TV stations have their own collection of local news, but it is unlikely that the public has access to them since there is not enough money to support an information and retrieval system for researchers.

COMPILED SUBJECT TAPES: CBS CONTROL OF GOVERNMENT ARCHIVES POLICY

At a communications conference in 1977, the former president of the Corporation for Public Broadcasting, Henry Loomis, addressed the audience. He was proud of the fact that PBS is television's book of public record for the Bert Lance hearings, which PBS covered gavel to gavel just as it had done during Watergate. It is impressive to have an electronic "book of public record," but it is more impressive that people do not have access to that book because public television is not organized for access. Nor was commercial television before 1973.

Until Paul Simpson challenged the networks by establishing Vanderbilt's Television News Archive, broadcasters operated our most advanced form of communication as if we lived at the dawn of history when books belonged to the privileged few, not only because they were expensive, fragile, and rare, but also because knowledge is power. Access to records is the heart of political accountability and the nub of the problem is compiled subject tapes: a tape that consists of spliced segments, all related to a particular subject. CBS has opposed systematically their production and it has persuaded the National Archives to sign an agreement with it that allows CBS to impose its policy on NA. The agreement is worded carefully so that the government conforms to CBS's ideas about contents, access procedures, use, and format.

There are two ways to look at network control over use of a government archival collection. The most generous interpretation is that progress has been made: at last, networks agree that television history should be available for research. CBS generously donates color cassettes of excellent quality, as well as their index, without which the collection would be of doubtful use. A less generous interpretation is that CBS's agreement with the National Archives has compromised the public interest by infringing on governmental authority in two ways: it unnecessarily limits public access, and it prevents the use of NA tapes for education in the classroom.

CBS infringes on governmental authority by dictating policy to the nation's archives with respect to what CBS materials it may and may not collect and how they may be used. (It is inconceivable that the *Washington Post* or the *New York Times* could limit the National Archives to collecting front-page news and a specified number of feature articles, and then tell the government under what conditions the material may be circulated.)

CBS limits public access severely as a result of its prohibition against compiled tapes. Television is a continuum that cannot be scanned, and the only feasible way to research a particular subject covered on TV is to use compiled tapes. CBS says that compilation by subject violates the integrity of the news by taking segments out of context and stitching together bits and pieces of information. This unsophisticated description by Richard Salant, former president of CBS news, is a definition of research as it is done every day by grammar school students, university professors, and by CBS journalists.

Consider the problem of researching how the commercial TV networks reported Wounded Knee on their evening news. The first telecast was on February 28, 1973 and the last was on May 9. That is nine weeks, give or take a couple of days, or approximately 67.5 hours of evening news (three networks' half-hour evening news programs, five nights a week for nine weeks is 67.5 hours, including commercials). Somewhere in those broadcasts there may or may not be segments about Wounded Knee. On most evenings there were. If CBS had been successful in persuading the Vanderbilt Television News Archive to accept the same agreement that it talked the National Archives into accepting, a researcher would have to watch 67.5 hours of television in order to see the relevant occasional segments. That is about ten seven-hour days to see TV news that a compiled tape will allow you to see in three hours. Think how costly this is in terms of the researcher's time, in terms of tying up a playback facility that other researchers need, in terms of people fetching and carrying all those cassettes, and if the researcher requests the cassettes by mail, think of the cost to ship that bulk of material! The CBS system wastes time, money, and material. It was conceived by someone who wants to prevent access under the guise of seeming cooperation.

Fortunately, however, the Vanderbilt Television News Archive has maintained its independence from network control. It did not sign a similar agreement with CBS. That is why the author was able to obtain from TNA a compiled tape of how each network had reported Wounded Knee on their evening news on tapes that ran for a total of three hours. This enables the researcher to study them easily, go back and forth, take notes, analyze visuals, and do the usual things that researchers do. The TNA tapes clearly identified each segment and its network of origin. The date and time that the segments were broadcast were also visible. That information cannot be erased and always shows on the screen. This helps to protect the networks' property.

In brief, CBS's policy against compiled tapes is clearly a means of preventing access. It is inappropriate for the networks to dictate policy to a government-run archive that is supported by public taxes. That policy, which is one more example of how broadcasters govern, should be rescinded and other archives should be forewarned about signing such agreements with CBS.

CBS further limits reasonable access to information by insisting that the National Archives respond to mail requests by sending tapes to institutions, not directly to the user, and that the user should be forbidden from taking the tape out of the institution to which tapes are sent. Automatically, this prevents use for educational purposes in a classroom. This is unfortunate. Today's students are, in large part, a product of the electronic age. They need specialized instruction in analyzing television, particularly since it affects behavior and value formation. But even if CBS did allow classroom use, that permission would be valueless without compiled tapes. Under the quarter system, college students have about 30 or 36 hours in a classroom. Professors cannot grope through 67.5 hours of uncompiled tapes in an orderly way and use the subject effectively to illustrate how the networks reported on Wounded Knee. CBS does make separate agreements with schools, allowing them to tape network news-as-aired for a fee (providing it is erased in 30 days). However, that still does not meet the need for compiled tapes in order to study televised history or to have reasonable access to the National Archives video collection. As for not letting the user take the tape out of the library (CBS is concerned that a user might duplicate the tape), this can be terribly inconvenient. If a researcher in Alaska borrows material from NA through the interlibrary loan system, and it is shipped to the nearest library, which does not have a playback facility, then the researcher effectively is denied access.

CBS sees compiled tapes as new documentaries that compete with network productions. They are particularly uneasy about the fact that the compiled tapes of the Television News Archive are returned to the collection in Nashville and other researchers might use them rather than make their own set of editorial judgments and compile other tapes. CBS probably knows a lot about this problem since they do the same thing every day with other media. If the *New York Times Magazine* commissions an extensive and expensive study on the energy crisis, which it then publishes, there is no reason why CBS cannot use part of it as well as several other sources to make another study. This is how books get written. This is how CBS produces its television documentaries and news specials. This is what we mean by a free flow of information. CBS's position is not a claim to copyright protection; it is a claim for censorship privileges, and in a democracy that special-interest claim must be denied in the name of a higher cause: freedom of the press. Possibly a National Archives user would duplicate, rebroadcast, or show publicly the NA tapes. But that possibility is not a mandate for repression. That is the risk that a free society takes in order to protect the public's interest in a democracy. There are few matters of greater importance than the need for access to an information source that is used by 75 percent of the people who inform themselves about public affairs, especially since 65 percent of those people use it as their only source of information and that, in turn, helps to guide their participation in the political process.

The key to accountability in broadcasting is television archives, in general, and compiled tapes in particular. Every other means of holding TV executives responsible for their actions, whether it be press councils, citizens groups, government regulation, or teaching electronic literacy, will be more effective if there are television archives whose policies make access possible.

8

POLICY CONSIDERATIONS

The government is the people and the people can organize to effect change. That cannot be said often enough. It is a myth that individuals are less important today than they were in the past. Communication systems have made people more important than ever before because they can know more and communicate with others in ways that were unknown when the United States was a fledgling country.

Television as government should be looked at carefully, and if adjustments need to be made they should not be undertaken by institutionalized government for all the obvious reasons that are encompassed in one: the medium's vast powers are too great a temptation for propagandists. Instead, press councils and citizens' groups should suggest policy in the public interest, not only with regard to access, but also with regard to program content. This was done successfully in 1978 and 1979 when certain sectors of the population acted to reduce violence and sex and to get more truth in advertising on television programs.

Television has done remarkable things for political participation in the United States. Although access to the air is distributed unfairly, more people have more access to a national audience, and consequently to authorities, than they ever had in the past. Americans are not politically apathetic. Read the papers and review the TV news from the 1960s to the present. People, just plain folks, are out there saying what it is that they want and insisting on getting it. We do have a problem with voting patterns, which seem to be in a consistent slump, but perhaps that is a function of unrealistic policies that govern the voting process. If so, change them. There is plenty of life in the body politic and there is every reason to be optimistic about the vitality of American democracy.

Obviously, the staggering cost of TV campaigns discourages some people from running for office, and it impedes others from competing effectively. Why not allow free air time for presidential candidates in the last two weeks of a campaign so they can reach a national audience? Local stations might work out similar arrangements for regional and local candidates. This suggestion is an old chestnut to pull out of the fire and it involves complex issues. But surely if creative people can put astronauts on the moon and film Jupiter, then they or some other creative minds can find a working solution for outrageously priced campaigns.

Electronic literacy is a pressing need. People must learn how to analyze what they see and hear on television. What is more important, they need to put electronic journalism in its proper perspective. Reporters and broadcast executives should not be allowed to teach the public that officials are guilty if they do not answer journalistic queries before the facts are known or the issues have been analyzed. Television news often means immediacy. Democracy often requires deliberation. Of the two, democracy and deliberation are more important. Ways must be found to protect them.

Broadcasters should get out of the government policy-making business and let TV archives work out their own policies based on users' needs. American democracy requires an informed citizenry. An informed citizenry requires access to compiled subject videotapes. This means we need television archives. It is a need, not a luxury. They should be funded by public taxes and by the hidden taxes that consumers pay for TV-advertised products. Broadcasters may not like to think of their profits as hidden taxes, but that is what they are and some of that money should go to work for the public whose property, the airwaves, is generating it.

Government must have access to the public. This is the modern age. Broadcasters cannot pretend that it is reasonable for Big Business (the commercial networks) to regulate government representatives' access to their constituents. In any event, all government-originated information should be labeled as such when it is broadcast instead of being passed off as news. If legislation is required to accomplish this, then it should be written because the public's right to know includes knowing whose bias is being seen and heard.

People want more and better television news. They have a right to it. They are paying for it. Television is used as a sole news source by many functional illiterates who, nonetheless, participate in the political process even if they do not vote. Therefore TV has a public interest obligation to cure itself of superficiality. Perhaps documentaries would be a suitable vehicle for investigative reporting. They have an excellent track record. However, broadcasters should not be hassled if they investigate controversial subjects. If the government

BIBLIOGRAPHY

VIDEOTAPES obtained from the Vanderbilt University Television News Archive include: *Wounded Knee:* A selection of segments from the evening news, as broadcast by ABC, NBC, and CBS from programs in November and December 1972 dealing with Indian protests, their takeover of the Bureau of Indian Affairs building, as well as selections from January, February, March, and April 1973, which reported the takeover of Wounded Knee. For additional information, see the Vanderbilt University Television News Archive's *Index and Abstracts; 1968 Democratic National Convention,* Chicago: This coverage was for the NBC broadcast on August 28, 1968; *Laos Incursion:* ABC, CBS, and NBC evening news, February 1971.

VIDEO SOURCES: The last name in the description is the key to obtaining the film. Consult the National Information Center for Educational Media, Educator's Purchasing Master, Lander's Film Reviews, and Educational Film Library Association for current addresses and other information.

Communications: The Wired World. Future technology includes interviews with Marshal McLuhan, Irving Kahn, et al. 1971, Document Associates.

Essay on Watergate. 59 minutes. Bill Moyers explores causes and effects. Produced before the resignation of President Nixon. 1973, Indiana University.

Hearts and Minds. 112 minutes. Our involvement in Vietnam. Interviews with General W. Westmoreland, former Secretary of Defense Clark Clifford, Senator William Fulbright, former presidential advisor Walter Rostow, Daniel Ellsberg, et al. RBC Films.

Interviews with My Lai Veterans. 22 minutes. Five My Lai veterans who participated in the massacre of Vietnamese civilians tell in detail what they did. 1971, New Yorker Films.

Journalism—Mirror, Mirror on the World? Analysis of news reporting of some peace marches by several different journalistic teams. Objectivity and the news. 1968, Indiana University.

Media: Massaging the Mind. 28 minutes. Discusses future media technology: lasers, satellites, holograms, home information centers, and effects of such changes. 1972, Document Associates.

Selling of the Pentagon—Rebuttal. 22 minutes. Richard Salant, president of CBS News, defends "Selling of the Pentagon" against charges of bias made by the Chairman of House Armed Services Citee, Secretary of Defense Melvin Laird and Vice President Agnew 1971, Carousel Films.

Selling of the Pentagon. 52 minutes. Exposé of Pentagon's public relations activities, which cost the nation $30-$190 million yearly. 1971, Carousel Films.

Shaping News for the Consumer. 17 minutes. Shows how a TV news story is put together. 1975, RFA Educational Media.

Sit-in. First lunch counter sit-in, May 10, 1960, Nashville. NBC White Paper Series. 1961, Contemporary Films/McGraw-Hill.

Six Hours to Deadline: A Free and Responsible Press. Process of going to press, analysis of social and ethical problems. 1962, Indiana University.

TV News: Behind the Scenes. Traces the preparation of New York City's "Eyewitness News". 1973, Encyclopedia Britannica Educational Corporation.

This Is Marshall McLuhan: The Medium Is the Massage. McLuhan presents his thoughts. 53 minutes. 1967, produced by NBC, Contemporary Films, McGraw-Hill.

Whole World Is Watching. 55 minutes. Discussion: bias on TV with David Brinkley, Walter Cronkite, John Fisher, Senator John O. Pastore. 1969, Indiana University.

BOOKS

Altheide, David L. *Creating Reality: How TV News Distorts Events.* Beverly Hills: Sage Publication, 1974.

Aronson, James. *Packaging the News: A Critical Survey of Press, Radio, TV.* New York: International Publishers 1971.

Aspen Notebook on Government and the Media. New York: Praeger, 1973.

Bagdikian, Ben H. *The Information Machines.* New York: Harper & Row, 1971.

Barnouw, Erik. *Tube of Plenty: The Evolution of American Television.* New York: Oxford University Press, 1975.

Barrett, Marvin, *Rich News, Poor News.* (The Alfred I Dupont-Columbia University Survey of Broadcast Journalism.) New York: Thomas Y. Crowell, 1978.

———. *Journalism: Moments of Truth?* New York: Columbia University, 1972/1973.

Barrett, Marvin, ed. *The Alfred I DuPont-Columbia University Survey of Broadcast Journalism, 1970-1971.* New York: Grosset & Dunlap, 1971.

Barron, Jerome A. *Freedom of the Press for Whom?: The Rise of Access to Mass Media.* Bloomington: University of Indiana Press, 1973.

Boorstin, Daniel. *The Republic of Technology: Reflections on Our Future Community.* New York: Harper & Row, 1978.

———. The Image. Harmondsworth, England: Penquin Books c-1961.

Bower, Robert T. *Television and the Public.* New York: Holt, Rinehart and Winston, 1973.

Bradlee, Benjamin C. *Conversations with Kennedy.* New York: Pocket Books, 1976.

Braestrup, Peter. *Big Story: How the American Press and TV Reported and Interpreted the Crisis of Tet 1968 in Vietnam and Washington,* vols. I, II. Boulder, Colorado: Westview Press, 1977.

Brown Les. *Television: The Business Behind the Box.* New York: Harcourt, Brace, Jovanovich, 1971.

Cater, Douglass. *The Fourth Branch of Government.* Boston: Houghton Mifflin, 1959.

Cirino, Robert. *Don't Blame the People: How the News Media Use Bias, Distortion and Censorship to Manipulate Public Opinion.* New York: Random House, 1971.

Dimond, Edwin. *The Tin Kazoo.* Cambridge, Mass.: MIT Press, 1975.

Doig, Ivan and Doig, Carol. *News: A Consumer's Guide.* Englewood Cliffs, N.J.: Prentice-Hall, 1972.

Ellul, Jacques. *The Technological Society.* New York: Vintage Books, 1964.

Epstein, Edward Jay. *News From Nowhere: Television and the News.* New York: Random House, 1973.

Fitzgerald, Frances. *Fire in the Lake.* New York: Vintage Books, 1972.

Friendly, Fred W. *The Good Guys, The Bad Guys and The First Amendment: Free Speech vs. Fairness in Broadcasting.* New York: Random House, 1975.

Groombridge, Brian. *Television and the People.* Baltimore, Md.: Penguin Books, 1972.

Hamilton, Alexander; Jay, John; and Madison, James. *The Federalist Papers*, vols. I, II. Washington: M. Walter Dunne, 1901.

Hulteng, John L. and Nelson, Roy Paul. *The Fourth Estate: An Informal Appraisal of the News and Opinion Media,* New York: Harper & Row, 1971.

Keogh, James. *President Nixon and the Press.* New York: Funk & Wagnalls, 1973.

Lasky, Victor. *It Didn't Start with Watergate.* New York: Dial Press, 1977.

Lipset, Seymour Martin. *Political Man: The Social Basis of Politics.* New York: Anchor Books, 1959.

Maddox, Brenda. *Beyond Babel: New Directions in Communications.* Boston: Beacon Press, 1974.

Mander, Jerry. *Four Arguments for the Elimination of Television.* New York: William Morrow, 1978.

McGinniss, Joe. *The Selling of the President 1968.* New York: Trident Press, 1969.

McLuhan, Marshall. *The Gutenberg Galaxy.* Toronto, Canada: University of Toronto, 1962.

———. *Understanding Media: The Extensions of Man.* New York: McGraw-Hill, 1964.

———. *Understanding Media: The Extensions of Man.* New York: McGraw-Hill, 1965.

———, Foire, and Quentin. *The Medium Is the Massage: An Inventory of Effects.* Harmondsworth, England: Penguin Books, 1967.

———. *War and Peace in the Global Village.* New York: Bantam Books, 1968.

Mickelson, Sig. *The Electric Mirror: Politics in an Age of Television.* New York: Dodd, Mead, 1972.

Minow, Newton N.; Martin, John Barthlow; and Mitchall, Lee M. *Presidential Television.* A Twentieth Century Fund Report. New York: Basic Books, 1973.

Mueller, Claus. *The Politics of Communication.* London: Oxford University Press, 1973.

Robinson, Glen O., ed. *Communications for Tomorrow: Policy Perspectives for the 1980's.* New York: Praeger, 1978.

Rubin, Bernard. *Media, Politics, and Democracy.* New York: Oxford University Press, 1977.

Rutland, Robert A. *The Newsmongers: Journalism in the Life of the Nation.* New York: Dial Press, 1973.

Sampson, Anthony. *The Seven Sisters: The Great Oil Companies and the World They Made.* New York: Viking, 1975.

Schlesinger, Arthur M., Jr. *The Imperial Presidency.* Boston: Houghton Mifflin, 1973.

Schmidt, Benno C., Jr. *Freedom of the Press vs. Public Access.* New York: Praeger, 1976.

Schorr, Daniel. *Clearing the Air.* New York: Houghton Mifflin, 1977.

Schram, Martin. *Running for President: A Journal of the Carter Campaign.* New York: Pocket Books, 1976.

Seiden, Martin H. *Who Controls the Mass Media?: Popular Myths and Economic Realities.* New York: Basic Books, 1974.

Small, William. *To Kill a Messenger: TV News and the Real World.* New York: Hastings House, 1970.

Sontag, Susan et al. *McLuhan Hot and Cool.* Harmondsworth, England: Penguin Books, 1968.

Stein, M.L. *Shaping the News: How the Media Functions in Today's World.* New York; Pocket Books, 1974.

Stein, Robert. *Media Power.* New York; Houghton Mifflin, 1972.

Tebbel, John. *The Media in America.* New York: Mentor Books, 1974.

Tocqueville, Alexis de. *Democracy in America.* Edited by J. P. Mayer and Kax Lerner. Translated by George Lawrence. New York: Harper & Row, 1966.

Twentieth Century Fund Commission. *Campaign Costs in the Electronic Era.* Voters' Time. New York: The Twentieth Century Fund, 1969.

Whale, John. *The Half-Shut Eye: TV and Politics in Britian and America.* London: Macmillan & Co., 1969.

White, Theodore. *The Making of the President 1968.* New York: Pocket Books, 1970.

Wise, David. *The Politics of Lying: Government, Deception, Secrecy, and Power.* New York: Random House, 1973.

———. *The American Police State.* New York: Random House, 1976.

DOCUMENTS AND UNPUBLISHED PAPERS

Adult Performance Level Final Report. Prepared under the direction of Dr. Norvell Northcutt, Division of Extension. University of Texas, Austin, August 1977. Study of functional illiteracy of the U.S. population.

Berman, Paul J., and Oettinger, Anthony G. *The Medium and the Telephone: The Politics of Information Resources.* Cambridge, Massachusetts: Harvard University Program on Information Technologies and Public Policy, 1976.

Cabinet Committee on Cable Communications. *The Cable: Report to the President.* Washington, D.C.: U.S. Government Printing Office, 1974.

CBS Transcripts: Wounded Knee: "CBS Evening News with Walter Cronkite," January 31, 1973–May 1, 1973. "60 Minutes" (excerpt) for Sunday March 4, 1973; "Face the Nation" November 26, 1972 (Guest: Peter MacDonald, chairman, Navaho Nation).

Congressional Quarterly Research Staff, *Watergate: Chronology of a Crisis,* vols. I, II. Edited by William B. Dickinson, Jr. Washington, D.C.: Congressional Quarterly, 1973.

Congressional Quarterly Research Staff. *Dollar Politics: The Issue of Campaign Spending,* vols. I, II Washington, D.C.: Congressional Quarterly, 1971.

Dobrovir, William et al. "The Offenses of Richard M. Nixon." Washington, D.C.: Public Issues Press, 1973.

Jacklin, Phil. "Toward a New Communications Act: Better than Fairness—Access" Unpublished paper, June 11, 1973, Department of Philosophy, San Jose State University.

Mosco, Vicent. "The Regulation of Broadcasting in the U.S.: A comparative analysis" (of FM, UHF, CATV, Subscription TV). Harvard University Program on Information Technologies and Public Policy. Cambridge, Massachusetts, 1975.

Nixon, President Richard. *Submission of Recorded Presidential Conversations to the Committee on the Judiciary of the House of Representatives.* Washington, D.C.: U.S. Government Printing Office, 1974.

Oettinger, Anthony G., and Shapiro, Peter D. "Information Industries in the U.S." Harvard University Program on Information Technologies & Public Policy. Cambridge, Massachusetts, 1975.

Powledge, Fred. "The Engineering of Restraint: The Nixon Administration and the Press." A report of the American Civil Liberties Union. Washington D.C.: Public Affairs Press, 1971.

Robinson, Michael J., and McPherson, Karen A. "Television News and the Presidential Nominating Process: The Case of Spring 1976." Unpublished paper.

Sheehan, Neil; Smith, Hedrick; Kenworthy, E.W.; and Butterfield, Fox. *The Pentagon Papers.* New York: Bantam Books, 1971.

U.S. Senate Committee on Commerce. "Overview of the Telecommunications Policy." Hearing before the subcommittee on Communications—93rd Congress, February 20, 1973. Serial #93-2. Washington, D.C. U.S. Government Printing Office, 1973. 135 pages.

"Wounded Knee 1973." Venceremos Publications, 1969 University Avenue, East Palo Alto, California. March 27, 1973. 23 pages.

ARTICLES

Adams, Hank. "The Wounded Knee Negotiations." *Indian Voice,* June-July 1973, pp. 5-7, 38-41, 44-46.

Agnew, Spiro. "The Power of the Press." In *The Mass Media Book.* Englewood Cliffs, N.J.: Prentice-Hall, 1972.

Barron, Jerome. "From Fairness to Access." In the *Alfred I. DuPont Survey of Broadcast Journalism, 1970-1971.* New York: Grosset & Dunlop, 1971. Pp. 133-140.

Bell, Daniel. "Technology, Nature and Society: The Viscissitudes of Three World Views and the Confusion of Realms." *The American Scholar,* Summer 1973.

Benard, Michael P. "Access to News Transcripts: Terribly Burdensome." *Columbia Journalism Review,* November-December 1976, p. 48.

Brown, Les. "Television vs. Progress." *International Review,* September 15, 1978, pp. 24-25.

Friedman, Mel. "A New Communications Act: The Debate Begins." *Columbia Journalism Review*, September-October 1978, pp. 40-43.

Friendly, Fred W. "Some Sober Second Thoughts on Vice President Agnew." In *The Mass Media Book.* Englewood Cliffs, N.J.: Prentice-Hill, 1972.

Goldstein, Paul. "Copyright and the First Amendment" *Columbia Law Review* 6, June 1970, pp. 983-1057.

Halberstam, David. "CBS: The Power and the Profits." *Atlantic,* January 1976, pp. 33-71, February 1976, pp. 52-91.

Hickey, Neil. "Was the Truth Burned at Wounded Knee?" *TV Guide,* December 1, 8, 15, 22, 1973.

Jacob, Charles E. "The Congressional Elections and Outlook." In *The Election of 1976.* New York: David McKay, 1977. Pp. 83-106.

Lang, Kurt and Engel, Gladys. "Televised Hearings: the Impact Out There." *Columbia Journalism Review,* November-December 1973, pp. 52-57.

McWilliams, Wilson Carey. "The Meaning of the Election." In *The Election of 1976.* New York: David McKay, 1977. Pp. 147-63.

Molotch, Harvey, and Lester, Marilyn. "Accidents, Scandals, and Routines: Resources for Insurgent Methodology." In *The TV Establishment*. Edited by Gaye Tuchmen. Englewood Cliff, N.J.: Prentice-Hall, 1974. Pp. 53-66.

Moyers, Bill D. "Press or Government, Who's Telling the Truth." In *The Mass Media Book*. Englewood Cliffs; N.J.: Prentice-Hall, 1972.

Novak, Michael. "The Inevitable Bias of Television." In *The Alfred I. DuPont Survey of Broadcast Journalism, 1970-1971*. New York: Grosset and Dunlop, 1971. Pp. 121-33.

Panitt, Merrill. "Television Today: The State of the Art." *TV Guide*, February 19, 1977 pp. 6-11.

———. "Network Power—Is it Absolute?" *TV Guide*, pp. 34-39.

———. "Programming for Profit." *TV Guide*, March 5, 1977, pp. 35-40.

Pool, Ithiel de Sola. "Newsmen and Statesmen: Adversaries or Cronies?" In *Aspen Notebook on Government and the Media*. New York: Praeger, 1973.

Reeves, Richard. "The Prime-Time President." *New York Tiems Magazine*, May 15, 1977, pp. 17-18.

Robinson, Michael J. "Television and American Politics, 1956-1976." *The Public Interest*, Summer 1977, pp. 3-39.

Royster, Vermont. "Thinking Things Over." *Wall Street Journal*, December 17, 1975.

Saldich, Anne. "Access to Television's Past: The Networks May Hide What Scholars Seek" *Columbia Journalism Review*, November-December 1976, pp. 46-51.

———. "Television, Education, Democratic aux USA." *Education 2000*, Paris, France. December 1978, pp. 51-57.

———. "Television News Archives: Broadcasting Enters an Era of Accountability" In *The Classroom and the Newsroom*. Robert Schmuhl, ed. The Poynter Center, Indiana University, 1979. Pp. 65-73.

Schreibman, Fay. "Television News Archives: A Guide to Major Collections." In *The Classroom and the Newsroom*. Edited by Robert Schmuhl. The Poynter Center, Indiana University 1979. Pp. 73-93.

Smith D. "Wounded Knee: The Media Coup d'etat." *Nation*, June 25, 1973, 806-9.

Tolchin, Martin. "An Old Poll Takes on the New President." *New York Times Magazine*, July 24, 1977, p. 6.

Tuchman, Gaye. "Introduction." In *The TV Establishment.* Edited by Gaye Tuchman. Englewood Cliffs, N.J.: Prentice-Hall, 1974. Pp. 1-41.

INDEX

ABC (American Broadcasting Company), 9, 10, 36, 84

Abernathy, Ralph, 14

access, 32, 34, 56, 59, 84, 88, 95, 100, 101, 106, (*see also* accountability, censorship, democracy, news, TV archives, TV as a corridor to power, Vanderbilt Television News Archive)

accountability, 77-78, 100-101, (*see also* Constitution of the U.S., democracy, First Amendment, TV accountability, TV Archives)

advertising on TV, 25, 29, 55, 56, 75; revenue 34, 76, 94 (*See also* TV, behavioral effects)

Agnew, Spiro, 77

Albert, Carl, 82, 86

"All in the Family," 26, 35, 55

American Indian Movement (AIM), 12, 13, 14, 16, 59 (*See also* manipulation, news, Wounded Knee)

American Television Arts & Sciences TV Archives, 105

apathy (*See* elections; *see also* audience, community, democracy pressure groups, Proposition 13, TV behavioral impact, violence)

archives (*see* television archives)

audience (*see* news, audience, Proposition 13, TV debates, Watergate)

authority, 23, 95; TV enhances its own authority, 61, 67; undermined by TV, 10, 89

Bank, Dennis, 17

Bill of Rights, 4

blacks, 59, 70

Boorstin, Daniel, 93, 98-99

Braestrup, Peter, 8

Bureau of Indian Affairs, 11-12, 13, 89 (*see also*, Indians, Wounded Knee)

CBS (Columbia Broadcasting System), 9, 10, 14, 15, 16, 72, 77, 78, 84, 101, 103, 104, 105, 106-107; sues Vanderbilt University Television News Archive, 65, 102, 105 (*see also* Paley, William, Salant, Richard, Vanderbilt University TV News Archives)

Cambodia, 6, 11 (*see also* censorship, Indo-China, Laos, Vietnam)

campaigns, 110 (*see also* campaigns, elections, Proposition 13)

Capricorn One, 78

Carnegie Commission on the Future of Public Broadcasting, 86, 87

Carter, Jimmy, 44, 81, 83-86

censorship, 4, 5, 6, 7, 8, 9, 10, 24, 30, 31, 65, 100 (*see also* TV archives, TV compiled tapes, TV, how it governs)

Chavez, Cesar, 59

Churchill, Winston, 47, 81

community (political), 13, 14, 18-19, 54, 57, 89, 93, 99

Congressional Record, 87

Connally, John, 44

Constitution of the United States, 4, 27,

61–62, 79, 93, 99
Corporation for Public Broadcasting, 76
    (see also public broadcasting)
credibility, 94; of TV, 13, 15, 23, 63, 65,
    73–74, 80–82, 89 (see also TV intimacy)
Cronkite, Walter, 9, 15, 26, 67, 84

Daley, Richard, 18
de Gaulle, Charles, 31, 78, 81–82
democracy, 49–50, 52, 61, 75, 78, 82, 83, 87,
    91, 95, 97–98, 109; accountability, 77,
    106; need for informed citizens, 36, 57,
    58, 65, 74; restructuring of 70; TV as a
    democratizing force, 57, 59; in Viet-
    nam, 6 (see also TV accountability, TV
    compiled tapes, Watergate)
Democratic Party, 1968 Convention riots,
    18–19
Diem, Ngo Dinh, 96
documentaries, 34, 38, 75, 111
docudramas, 35

Eagleton, Thomas, 46–47
Eisenhower, Dwight D., 92, 96
elections, 44; campaigns, 110; Presidential
    debates, 37–38, 51; voter turnout, 30,
    35–36 (see also interest politics)
equal time, 34
Ervin, Sam, 99
Evans, M. Stanton, 16, 112

FBI (Federal Bureau of Investigation), 14
Federal Communications Commission
    (FCC), 24, 83
First Amendment, 5, 26–28, 61–63, 66, 88
Ford, Gerald, 83
"free" TV, 68, 111
free speech messages, 32 (see also access)
Freedom of the Press, 62 (see also First
    Amendment Constitution of the U.S.)
French TV, 31, 78, 81–82 (see also deGaulle,
    Charles)
Frost, David, 24, 98

Garth, David, 84
government, diplomacy by TV, 33–34,

House of Representatives financing a
    government press, 5; secrecy, 28–29
Government Printing Office, 87
Graham, Katharine, 97

handicapped demonstrations, 57
Harris, Louis, 83
Harris Survey, January 1978, 37

illiteracy (see literacy)
Indians, American, 11–18, 59, 89 (see also
    Wounded Knee)
Indochina, 4–11; demonstrations against
    the U.S., 9, 10, 89–90 (see also Cambo-
    dia, Laos, Vietnam)
International Federation of Television
    Archives, 102
International Studies Association, 101
interest politics (see pressure groups)
interviews, 33–34
investigative reporting, 34, 36

Jacklin, Phillip, 32
Jarvis-Gann initiative (see Proposition 13)
Johnson, Lyndon B., 7, 96
Justice Department, U.S., 15 (see also
    Wounded Knee)

Kennedy, John F, 6, 96
Klein, Paul, 84

Lance, Bert, 24, 106
Laos, 6, 9, 10, 11 (see also censorship, Indo-
    China, Vietnam)
Legum, Colin, 88
Library of Congress Motion Picture and
    Recorded Sound Division, 101, 103
licensing broadcasters, 22–48
Lincoln, Abraham, 47
literacy, electronic, 29, 79, 103, 110; linear,
    29, 53–57, 69–71 (see also TV archives)
Loomis, Henry, 106

"MacNeil/Lehrer Report," 33, 36, 37
McCarthy, Joseph, 32
McGovern, George, 46–47

McGinniss, Joseph, 77, 78
McGrory, Mary, 97
McLuhan, Marshall, 1, 2, 3, 4, 14; TV as a medium hot on cool, 17
massacre, My Lai, 7, 8, 9; Wounded Knee 1890, 12
Mead, Margaret, 51
media politics, 12, 13, 14, 17-18, 54, 56, 59-60 (see also news manipulation, street politics, TV teaches politics of violence, Wounded Knee)
migrant workers, 59
Mitchell, John, 97
Murrow, Edward R., 32
Museum of Broadcasting, 101, 104
My Lai, cover-up, 8, 9; massacre, 7; public response, 8

NBC (National Broadcasting Company), exacerbates Chicago 1968 violence, 18, 84, 105
National Academy of Television Arts and Sciences' Archives, 101
National Archives, audiovisual division, 101, 103, 105, 106, 108
Network (motion picture), 67
news, archives, 64; catalyst for action, 4; coverage of U.S. Indo-China War, 8; creating the news, 4, 5; daytime news programs, 35; immediacy, 28-29; magazines, 32-33; manipulation, 26, 56, 60, 72, 96; objectivity, 24, 71, 74, 76; scope, 33, 70; superficiality, 29, 36, 57-58, 67 (see also CBS, National Archives, Vanderbilt University Television News Archives, Wounded Knee)
news, audience, 37, 38, 58, 62
Nixon, Richard, 9, 10, 14, 24, 32, 33, 92, 96, 98; administration, 9, 10, 14, 15, 76, 98, 99, 101; strategy for controlling the press, 77, 93 (see also Wounded Knee, Watergate)

objectivity (see news, objectivity; Nixon, Richard, strategy for controlling the press)

Office of Telecommunications Policy, 77
O'Neill Jr., Thomas P. ("Tip"), 85, 86
order, civic 23, 28

Paley, William, 72, 78, 104
Parents Teachers Association, 56
political participation, 3, 4 (see also apathy, elections)
politicizing effects of TV (see TV politicizing effects, advertising)
political satire, 35
political speeches, 34
Powers, Francis Gary, 96
presidential coverage, 34-35, 38, 82-86, 95
presidential press conferences, 33, 85
presidential trips, 33
press, Federal Government's press, 4, 34, 35, 86; free press, 4, 55, 92, manipulation of, 14, 15-16, 17, 92, 96-97
pressure groups, 30, 50, 87, 97 (also called interest politics)
propaganda, 75, 78, 86-88, 96-97, 111
Proposition 13 (Jarvis-Gann initiative), 51-52
public broadcasting, 86, 105; presidential access, 34; Nixon strategy to control, 76; Watergate, 96
public opinion, manipulation of, 17, 24, 55 (see also censorship, demonstrations, Wounded Knee)

Reasoner, Harry, 10, 36
Ridenhour, Ron, 7, 9
right to reply, 34
rights, human, 10
Roosevelt, Franklin D., 82, 92
Royster, Vermont, 93

Salant, Richard, 16, 78, 204
Sampson, Anthony, 73
Santayana, George, 95
Schieffer, Robert, 84
Schorr, Dan, 72, 78
secrecy, 28, 29
Seiden, Martin, 69
"Selling of the Pentagon," 34, 75

Selling of the President (book), 77
Sevareid, Eric, 15, 16
Simpson, Paul, 101, 106 (*see also* Vanderbilt University Television News Archive)
Sirica, John, 94, 99
Small, William, 70
Smith, Howard K., 10
street politics, 4, 30, 54, 56 (*see also* interest politics, media politics, pressure groups)
Suratt, S., 105
symbols, political significance, 54, 60

technology, socio-political consequences, 53, 68, 79, 80, 90, 104
television, abuse of its power, 63, 100, (subject tapes, 103–104); accountability, 61, 63–66, 69, 77–78, 100–101, 103–104, 106; antidotes to power, 23, 79, 91; archives, 63, 64, 79, 101–106, 110; behavioral impact, 53–57, 71, 74–75, 90, 99, 110; as big business, 63, 64, 65, 88; corridor to power, 22–23, 57, 59; cross-ownership, 68–69; debates, 80; distortion of reality, 71–73; how it governs, 22–48, 64, 79, 103, 106, 109; information source, 1, 57–58, 111; intimacy, 80 (*see also* credibility); international diplomacy, 33–34; investigative reporting, 18, 111; limitations, 66–67; network affiliates, 76; manipulation of, 15, 59–60, 78; personalizes power, 80–91; political programs (categories of), 31–36; public

service, 22–23, 27, 68, 75, 94, 109, 111; profits, 5, 86, 94, 111; regulation, 26–28, 75–77, 79, 86–87, 97, 109; teaching a politics of violence, 9, 10, 13, 18, 53, 56, 59, 71, 74–75, 89; unique powers, 25–26, 36, 63, 66, 69, 80; (*see also* authority, censorship, community, credibility, order, violence, Watergate)
Television News Study Center, 101, 102
Thieu, Nguyen Van, 31
tyranny, 61–79 (*see also* Constitution of the U.S., First Amendment, freedom of the press)

Vanderbilt University Television News Archive, 1, 63, 100–101, 102, 105, 107; sued by CBS, 65
video research, compiled subject tapes, 1
Vietnam, 5, 6, 8, 9, 10, 95–96; French experience in, 6; massacre, 7 (*see also* Cambodia, censorship, Indo-China, Laos)
violence and TV, 2, 4, 9, 10, 13, 14, 17, 18, 19, 53, 56–57, 59, 71 (*see also* TV teaches a politics of violence)

Walters, Barbara, 36
Watergate, 13, 32, 38, 76–77, 92–93
Watts, California, 18, 19
Wiley, Richard E., 24
Wounded Knee, 11–18, 59, 60, 107–108 (*see also* media politics, violence)

ABOUT THE AUTHOR

Anne Rawley Saldich, a political sociologist, specializes in media and politics. While earning her doctorate at the Sorbonne she wrote a dissertation under the direction of Raymond Aron, about de Gaulle's use of television as an instrument of power. She has taught international relations, American government, and Electronic Democracy at the University of California, Berkeley. She is a member of the International Institute of Communications (London).

Dr. Saldich has written for several communications magazines, including the *Columbia Journalism Review*, *InterMedia* (London) the *Irish Broadcasting Review*, and the French journal *l'Education 2000* (Paris).

After living abroad for several years, in England and France, her home is now in Palo Alto, California.